BOOK 1

World Link

Developing English Fluency

Susan Stempleski
Nancy Douglas • James R. Morgan

THOMSON

Australia · Canada · Mexico · Singapore · Spain · United Kingdom · United States

World Link 1, **Student Book**
Susan Stempleski

Nancy Douglas • James R. Morgan

Publisher: Christopher Wenger
Director of Marketing: Amy Mabley
Director of Product Development: Anita Raducanu
Acquisitions Editor: Mary Sutton-Paul
Sr. Marketing Manager: Eric Bredenberg
Developmental Editor: Paul MacIntyre
Production Manager: Sally Cogliano
Production Editor: Tan Jin Hock

Sr. Print Buyer: Mary Beth Hennebury
Compositor: Christopher Hanzie, Ronn Lee, TYA Inc.
Project Manager: Christopher Hanzie
Photo Researcher: Christopher Hanzie, Ronn Lee
Illustrator: Raketshop Design Studio (Philippines),
Cover/Text Designer: Christopher Hanzie, TYA Inc.
Printer: C&C Offset Printing Co., Ltd.
Cover Image: TYA Inc. PhotoDisc, Inc.

Printed in China
5 6 7 8 9 10   08 07

For more information contact Thomson Heinle
25 Thomson Place, Boston, MA 02210 USA, or you can visit our Internet site at elt.thomson.com

For permission to use material from this text or product, submit a request online at http://www.thomsonrights.com Any additional questions about permissions can be submitted by email to thomsonrights@thomson.com

ISBN-13: 978-0-8384-0662-5
ISBN-10: 0-8384-0662-9
Library of Congress Number: 2004094088

Photo Credits

Unless otherwise stated, all photos are from PhotoDisc, Inc. Digital Imagery © copyright 2005 PhotoDisc, Inc. and TYA Inc. Photos from other sources: page 9: Filippo Monteforte/EPA/Landov (D. Beckham); page 10: David Maris/EPA/Landov (Y. Ming), WENN/Landov (M. Gray), Reuters/Juan Carlos Ulate/Landov (L. Pavarotti), Kevin Lamarque/Reuters/Landov (M. Sharapova); page 11: Hubert Boesl/DPA/Landov (B. Affleck), Francis Specker/Landov (L. Tyler), EPA/David Cheskin/Landov (Prince William), Reuters/Srdjan Alvulovic/Landov (V. Williams), Manjunath Kiran/EPA/Landov (E. Iglesias), UPI Photo/Laura Cavanaugh/Landov (A. Judd), Ethan Miller/Reuters/Landov (W. Judd), EPA/John Reilly/Landov (J. Iglesias Jr.), EPA/Eddy Rischh/Landov (S. Williams), John Hrusa/EPA/Landov (Prince Harry), John-Marshall Mantel/CORBIS (M. Tyler), Rune Hellestad/Corbis (C. Affleck); page 19: Douglas Fisher/ALAMY (middle left), Dynamic Graphics Group/IT Stock Free/ALAMY (middle right); page 28: ML Sinabaldi/CORBIS (left), Sandy Felsenthal/CORBIS (middle), Ameet Pean Pierre/CORBIS SYGMA (right); page 29: C. Wenger/Thomson; page 36: Image Source Limited/Index Stock Imagery (bottom right); page 37: Oote Boe/Alamay (top left), Royalty Free/CORBIS (middle left); page 43: Stephen Saks Photography/ALAMY (top), Jon Bower/ALAMY (bottom); page 48: Yen-Wen Lu/ALAMY; page 51: oote boe/Alamy (bottom left), Conner/Index Stock Imagery (bottom right), Jeff Greenberg/Alamy (bottom middle); page 52: Lester Lefkowitz/CORBIS (leg), Timeline Images/ALAMY (mannequin), William Whitehurst/CORBIS (eye); page 63: Alison Wright/CORBIS (A.S. Kyi), Steve Reigate/EPA/Landov (Queen Elizabeth), DPA/Landov (A. Einstein), Toni Garriga/EPA/Landov (R. Crowe); page 80: Jim Zuckerman/CORBIS (left), Swim Ink/CORBIS (Superman), Tom Gilbert/AP Photo (Anne Frank), Bettmann/CORBIS (M. Gandhi); page 81: Bettmann/CORBIS (A. Lincoln), Bettmann/CORBIS (M.L. King), Bettmann/CORBIS (J.F. Kennedy); page 82: Columbia/Sony/The Kobal Collection/Chuen, Chan Kam (top), Warner Bros. (bottom); page 83: Bettmann/CORBIS (top), Bettmann/CORBIS (bottom); page 84: 20th Century Fox/The Kobal Collection (top), Bettmann/CORBIS (bottom); page 85: Marshall John/CORBIS SYGMA (Bono), Bassouls Sophie/CORBIS SYGMA (A. Roy), Bill Greenblatt/UPI/Landov (O. Winfrey); page 87: Artists Without Borders (middle); page 102: Lynn Goldsmith/CORBIS (B. Marley); page 103: Gabe Palmer/CORBIS; page 107: Jose Luis Pelaez/CORBIS (top left) CORBIS; page 109: Getty Images (middle); page 114: Chip East/Reuters/Landov (top left), Reuters/Mike Segar/Landov (top right), Ted Soqui/CORBIS (middle left), Rune Hellestad/CORBIS (middle right), Bettmann/CORBIS (bottom right); page 118: Fred Prouser/Reuters/Landov; page 119: Steve Raymer/CORBIS (left), Anchorage Daily News/Associated Press (center), Reuters/Mike Blake/Landov (right); page 120: Royalty Free/CORBIS (left); page 121: Michael Crabtree/Reuters/CORBIS (top), Associated Press/AP (bottom left), Associated Press/AP (bottom right); page 124: Dreamworks LCC/The Kobal Collection (SHREK), Hypnotic/Universal Pictures/The Kobal Collection (Bourne Identity), Miramax/Universal/The Kobal Collection (Bridget Jones's Diary), Universal/The Kobal Collection (West Side Story), Mirsch-7 Arts/United Artists/The Kobal Collection (Dracula), Lucasfilm/The Kobal Collection (Star Wars: The Phantom Menace); page 125: Paul King/Alamy (top), Walt Disney Pictures/PIXAR (Finding Nemo), DNA/Figment/Fox/The Kobal Collection (28 Days Later), Lions Gate Films (Girl with a Pearl Earring); page 127: David Petty/Index Stock Imagery (center), 20th Century Fox/Paramount/The Kobal Collection (bottom); page 128: New Zealand Film Commission/The Kobal Collection; page 129: MGM/The Kobal Collection (left), Warner Bros./The Kobal Collection/Hamill, Brian (right); page 130: Lisa O'Connor/ZUMA/CORBIS (top), Columbia/Sony/The Kobal Collection/Chuen, Chan Kam (bottom); page 131: Dreamworks LCC/The Kobal Collection (top), 20th Century/Zanuck Co./The Kobal Collection/Emerson, Sam (bottom); page 133: Cristaldi Films/Films Ariane/The Kobal Collection

Acknowledgments

We would firstly like to thank the educators who provided invaluable feedback throughout the development of the *World Link* series:

Byung-kyoo Ahn, Chonnam National University; Elisabeth Blom, Casa Thomas Jefferson; Grazyna Anna Bonomi; Vera Burlamaqui Bradford, Instituto Brasil-Estados Unidos; Araceli Cabanillas Carrasco, Universidad Autónoma de Sinaloa; Silvania Capua Carvalho, State University of Feira de Santana; Tânia Branco Cavaignac, Casa Branca Idiomas; Kyung-whan Cha, Chung-Ang University; Chwun-li Chen, Shih Chien University; María Teresa Fátima Encinas, Universidad Iberoamericana-Puebla and Universidad Autónoma de Puebla; Sandra Gaviria, Universidad EAFIT; Marina González, Instituto de Lenguas Modernas; Frank Graziani, Tokai University; Chi-ying Fione Huang, Ming Chuan University; Shu-fen Huang (Jessie), Chung Hua University; Tsai, Shwu Hui (Ellen), Chung Kuo Institute of Technology and Commerce; Connie R. Johnson, Universidad de las Américas-Puebla; Diana Jones, Instituto Angloamericano; Annette Kaye, Kyoritsu Women's University; Lee, Kil-ryoung, Yeungnam University; David Kluge, Kinjo Gakuin University; Nancy H. Lake; Hyunoo Lee, Inha University; Amy Peijung Lee, Hsuan Chuang College; Hsiu-Yun Liao, Chinese Culture University; Yuh-Huey Gladys Lin, Chung Hua University; Eleanor Occeña, Universitaria de Idiomas, Universidad Autónoma del Estado de Hidalgo; Laura Pérez Palacio, Tecnológico de Monterrey; Doraci Perez Mak, União Cultural Brasil-Estados Unidos; Mae-Ran Park, Pukyong National University; Joo-Kyung Park, Honam University; Bill Pellowe, Kinki University; Margareth Perucci, Sociedade Brasileira de Cultura Inglesa; Nevitt Reagan, Kansai Gaidai University; Lesley D. Riley, Kanazawa Institute of Technology; Ramiro Luna Rivera, Tecnológico de Monterrey, Prepa; Marie Adele Ryan, Associação Alumni; Michael Shawback, Ritsumeikan University; Kathryn Singh, ITESM; Grant Trew, Nova Group; Michael Wu, Chung Hua University

---

A great many people participated in the making of the *World Link* series. In particular I would like to thank the authors, Nancy Douglas and James Morgan, for all their hard work, creativity, and good humor. I would also like to give special thanks to the developmental editor Paul MacIntyre, whose good judgment and careful attention to detail were invaluable. Thanks, too, to publisher Chris Wenger, and all the other wonderful people at Thomson/Heinle who have worked on this project. I am also very grateful to the many reviewers around the world, whose insightful comments on early drafts of the *World Link* materials were much appreciated.
Susan Stempleski

We'd like to extend a very special thank you to two individuals at Thomson/Heinle: Chris Wenger for spearheading the project and providing leadership, support and guidance throughout the development of the series, and Paul MacIntyre for his detailed and insightful editing, and his tireless commitment to this project. We also offer our sincere thanks to Susan Stempleski, whose extensive experience and invaluable feedback helped to shape the material in this book.

Thanks also go to those on the editorial, production, and support teams who helped to make this book happen: Anita Raducanu, Sally Cogliano, David Bohlke, Christine Galvin-Combet, Lisa Geraghty, Carmen Corral-Reid, Jean Pender, Rebecca Klevberg, Mary Sutton-Paul, and their colleagues in Asia and Latin America.

I would also like to thank my parents, Alexander and Patricia, for their love and encouragement. And to my husband Jorge and daughter Jasmine—thank you for your patience and faith in me. I couldn't have done this without you!
Nancy Douglas

I would also like to thank my mother, Frances P. Morgan, for her unflagging support and my father, Lee Morgan Jr., for instilling the love of language and learning in me.
James R. Morgan

World Link Level 1   *Scope and Sequence*

Reading & Writing	Language Link	Communication

		Unit 1
"Celebrity doubles": Reading about people who look like celebrities	Review of the simple present	"Find someone who . . .": Asking questions to find classmates with various interests and qualities
"Guess who?": Writing about a classmate	Describing people	"Family photos": Matching members of famous families

		Unit 2
"World Greetings": Reading about gestures in three countries	Review of the present continuous	"High school reunion": Role-playing people at a high school reunion
"Smiling in e-mail": Writing an e-mail using smileys and abbreviations	Object pronouns	"Pantomime": Playing a charade-style guessing game about actions

		Unit 3
"Garage sale bargains": Reading about bargain hunting at garage sales	Count and noncount nouns with *some* and *any*	"Island Survivor!": Choosing items to take on a survival trip to an island
"My favorite place to shop": Writing about a favorite place to shop	*Some/any; much/many; a lot of*	"Shopping spree": Making a list of things a student needs for an apartment

Review: Units 1–3 32

		Unit 4
"The best cities to live in": Reading an article about two great cities to live in	Prepositions of place	"A new neighborhood": Talking about ways of improving a neighborhood
"My city": Writing about a city you know	*How much/how many*	"Hosting the World Cup": Discussing the issues involved in hosting a World Cup soccer match

		Unit 5
"Lost and found": Reading an article about strange lost items	Connecting sentences with *but, or, so*	"Where should I go?": Choosing a vacation destination for a classmate
"Newspaper ad": Writing a newspaper ad about a lost item	*Whose*; possessive pronouns; *belong to*	"Are we compatible?": Taking a travel partner compatibility survey

		Unit 6
"What's your personality type?": Reading about four personality types	Verb + noun; verb + infinitive	"Who said that?": Guessing classmates' identities on the basis of their survey answers
"What are you like?": Writing a description of your personality	*How often . . . ?*; frequency expressions	"Personality quiz": Taking a quiz to determine your personality type

Review: Units 4–6 66

Scope and Sequence **v**

	Vocabulary Link	Listening	Speaking & Pronunciation

Reading & Writing	Language Link	Communication
"A lifetime dream": Reading about two people and their career dreams	*Like to* vs. *would like to*	"Bad habits": Role-playing a person with bad habits and giving the person advice
"My dream": Writing about the dream of a lifetime	The future with *be going to*	"Plans for the future": Asking and answering questions about the future
"Making a difference": Reading about the work of "Artists Without Borders"	The past tense of *be*	"Who was she?": Playing a game to discover the identity of a person from the past
"My hero": Writing about a hero	The simple past: regular verbs	"Hero of the Year": Choosing a person to be named "Hero of the Year."
"The meaning of dreams": Reading an article about the meaning of dreams	The simple past: irregular verbs	"Early memories": Recalling and sharing early childhood memories
"A strange dream": Writing about a strange dream	The simple past: question forms	"The house in my dream": Discovering personality traits through a dream house description
"Exam stress: What can I do?": Reading an advice column about exam stress	The imperative	"Health posters": Making a poster to increase health awareness
"A remedy for stress": Writing about how you relieve stress	*When*-clauses	"Stress survey": Taking a survey to determine whether you are generally calm or easily stressed.
"Two amazing achievements": Reading about two amazing people	Talking about skills and talents with *can* and *could*	"Talent search!": Discovering the hidden talents of your classmates
"An amazing experience": Writing about an amazing experience	Connecting ideas with *because*	"Thirteen things to do": Discussing things to do before the age of 70
"Movie remakes": Reading an article about two movie remakes	*-ing/-ed* adjectives	"Movie reviews": Reviewing and discussing a movie you saw recently
"My favorite movie": Writing about your favorite movie of all time	The present continuous as future	"Better the second time?": Planning a movie remake

New Friends, New Faces

Lesson A | Meeting new people

1 Vocabulary Link

Online pen pals

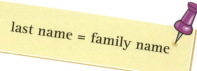
last name = family name

A Look at Silvia's website. Complete the website with the words in the box.

1. first name
2. languages
3. age
4. city
5. interests
6. country
7. e-mail address
8. occupation
9. last name

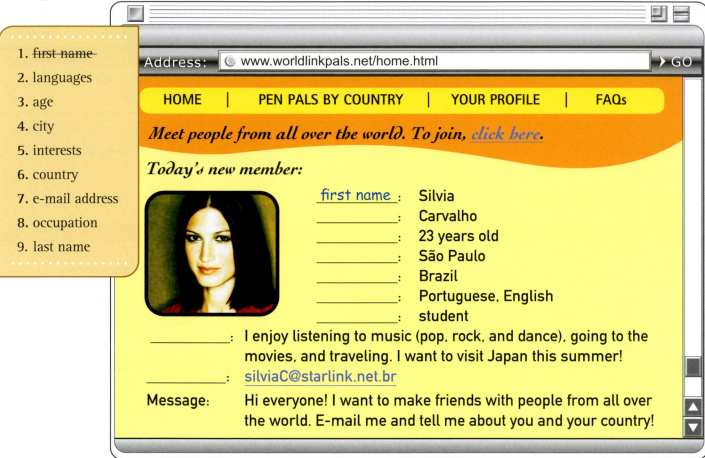

Address: www.worldlinkpals.net/home.html ❯ GO

HOME | PEN PALS BY COUNTRY | YOUR PROFILE | FAQs

Meet people from all over the world. To join, click here.

Today's new member:

<u>first name</u> : Silvia
_____ : Carvalho
_____ : 23 years old
_____ : São Paulo
_____ : Brazil
_____ : Portuguese, English
_____ : student
_____ : I enjoy listening to music (pop, rock, and dance), going to the movies, and traveling. I want to visit Japan this summer!
_____ : silviaC@starlink.net.br
Message: Hi everyone! I want to make friends with people from all over the world. E-mail me and tell me about you and your country!

B Match the questions with the answers.

1. _____ What's your name?
2. _____ Do you speak English?
3. _____ Where are you from?
4. _____ What do you do?
5. _____ What do you do for fun?
6. _____ How old are you?
7. _____ What's your e-mail address?

a. I'm 23.
b. I'm Silvia Carvalho.
c. Yes, and I also speak Portuguese.
d. São Paulo, Brazil.
e. I'm a student.
f. It's silviaC@starlink.net.br.
g. I like listening to music, going to the movies, and traveling.

In some countries, it's not polite to ask a person's age.

C **Pair work.** Use the questions in **B** to interview a partner.

2 Listening

Hi, I'm Fiona.

 A Listen to three people from the pen pals website.
Match the name of the speaker with his or her interest. (CD 1, Track 1)

a. Hiromi   **b.** Miguel   **c.** Fiona

 B Listen again. Answer the questions about the people.
Check (✓) the correct box. (CD 1, Track 2)

Who . . .	Hiromi	Miguel	Fiona
1. lives in Tokyo?	✓	☐	☐
2. is Australian?	☐	☐	☐
3. is from Mexico?	☐	☐	☐
4. is 19?	☐	☐	☐
5. is 24?	☐	☐	☐

Who . . .	Hiromi	Miguel	Fiona
6. is 28?	☐	☐	☐
7. is a math teacher?	☐	☐	☐
8. is a graphic artist?	☐	☐	☐
9. studies computers?	☐	☐	☐

3 Pronunciation

Question intonation review

ask&ANSWER

Do you like movies? soccer? comic books?
What other interests do you have?

 A Listen to the questions. Notice the rising [↗] or falling [↘] intonation. (CD 1, Track 3)

1. Are you from Seoul? [↗]   Where are you from? [↘]
2. Do you have a brother? [↗]   What's his name? [↘]

 B Listen to the questions. Write [↗] or [↘] . (CD 1, Track 4)

1. What do you do? _____   4. When does class end? _____
2. Is the teacher from England? _____   5. Do you like Italian food? _____
3. Do you have brothers and sisters? _____   6. Who's your favorite singer? _____

C **Pair work.** Practice asking and answering the questions in **B** with a partner.

Lesson A • Meeting new people   **3**

4 Speaking

Nice to meet you.

 A Mariana and Danny live in the same apartment building. Are they meeting for the first time? Listen to their conversation. **(CD 1, Track 5)**

Mariana:	Hi. My name is Mariana. I'm in apartment 201.
Danny:	Hi, Mariana. I'm Danny. I'm in 302. It's nice to meet you.
Mariana:	Nice to meet you, too.
Danny:	So, are you a student, Mariana?
Mariana:	Yeah, I study music at NYU.
Danny:	That's interesting.
Mariana:	What do you do, Danny?
Danny:	I'm a student at Hunter College. I also work in an art gallery.

 B **Pair work.** Practice the conversation. Then practice with *your* information.

C **Group work.** Introduce yourself to four classmates. Then ask about their names and occupations. Complete the chart with their information. Use the Useful Expressions to help you.

Useful Expressions:	
Introducing yourself	**Asking about occupations**
A: My name is Mariana. *or* I'm Mariana. B: (It's) Nice to meet you. A: (It's) Nice to meet you, too.	A: What do you do? B: I'm a music student.

Name	Occupation(s)
Mariana	student (studies music)
1. _____	_____
2. _____	_____
3. _____	_____
4. _____	_____

 D **Pair work.** Tell a new partner about the classmates you talked to in part **C**.

Mariana is a student. She studies music.

5 Language Link

Review of the simple present

I/you/we/they	he/she
speak	speaks
study	studies
teach	teaches
have	has
do	does

A Steffi is writing about herself and her classmate.
Read the sentences. Write the correct form of each verb.

Monika and Me

Monika **(1. be)** ___is___ my classmate. We **(2. be)** _____ different in many ways.
I **(3. be)** _____ an only child. Monika **(4. have)** _____ two brothers and a sister.
I **(5. live)** _____ with my family. Monika **(6. live)** _____ in her own apartment. We
both go to Sonoma State University, but I **(7. study)** _____ English Literature.
Monika **(8. study)** _____ business. I **(9. not have)** _____ a job, but Monika
(10. work) _____ at a café on the weekend. I **(11. love)** _____ dance music, but
Monika **(12. not like)** _____ dance music. She **(13. listen to)** _____ jazz or
classical music.

B **Pair work.** Study the chart. Then answer the *yes/no* questions below with a partner. Use short answers.

	Yes/No Questions	Yes Answers	No Answers
With *be*	Are you in this class?	Yes, I am.	No, I'm not.
With other verbs	Do you speak English?	Yes, I do.	No, I don't.
With *be*	Is she in this class?	Yes, she is.	No, she isn't.
With other verbs	Does she speak English?	Yes, she does.	No, she doesn't.

1. Is Steffi an only child?   __Yes, she is_____.
2. Does Steffi study business? _____.
3. Do Monika and Steffi go to the same university? _____.
4. Does Monika have a job? _____.
5. Are Steffi and Monika different? _____.

C **Pair work.** Read the answers below. Write the questions. Then take turns asking and answering them.

1. What __does Steffi study_____? Steffi studies English Literature.
2. Where _____? Monika works at a café.
3. Who _____? Steffi lives with her family.
4. Where _____? Monika lives in an apartment.
5. What _____? Steffi goes to the clubs on the weekend.
6. When _____? Monika watches TV on the weekend.

D Think of two *yes/no* questions to ask your partner. You can ask about school, family, hobbies, job, and
favorites. For each *yes/no* question, think of a *wh-*question to ask.

E **Pair work.** Interview your partner.

> Are you a student?
> Where do you go to school?

6 Communication

Find someone who . . .

A **Class activity.** For each item in the chart, ask the question and find a person who answers *Yes.*
Write his or her name. Then ask one more question and write some extra information.

Find someone who . . .	Classmate's name	Extra information
1. has a part-time job.		
2. travels sometimes.		
3. likes listening to music.		
4. is a university student.		
5. plays soccer.		
6. has a sister.		
7. goes to clubs on the weekend.		
8. has a dog or cat.		
9. drives a car.		
10. eats breakfast every day.		
11. dreams in English.		
12. watches movies every week.		
13. has an e-mail address.		
14. is an only child.		

Do you have a part-time job?

Yes, I do.

What do you do?

I work in a coffee shop.

B **Pair work.** Tell a classmate about the people in your chart.

World Link

According to a U.S. survey, the most common question asked among people meeting for the first time is: *What do you do?*

New Friends, New Faces

Lesson B | What does he look like?

---

1 Vocabulary Link

He's in his fifties.

A **Pair work.** Complete the sentences about each person in the family photo. Use the words in the box.

Age	Height
young	tall
in her/his 20s, 30s, 40s	average height
elderly (70+)	short
Weight	**Eye color**
thin	blue
slim	green
average weight	brown
heavyset	dark
Hairstyle	**Hair color**
long	black
short	(light/dark) brown
straight	blond
curly	gray
spiky	red

1. Emilio is ___in his fifties___. He is ___tall___ —about 182 cm. He is ___average weight___.
   He has ___brown___ eyes. He has ___short___, ___curly___, ___gray___ hair.

2. Kathy is _____. She is _____. She is _____. She has _____ eyes.
   She has _____, _____, _____ hair.

3. Michael is _____. He is _____. He is _____. He has _____ eyes.
   He has _____, _____, _____ hair.

4. Alexis and Ashley are _____. They are _____. They are _____.
   They have _____ eyes. They have _____, _____, _____ hair.

B **Pair work.** Look again at the picture. Answer the questions with a partner.

1. Who does Michael look like?   He looks like ___his father___.
2. Who does Ashley look like?   She looks like _____. They're twins.
3. Who do you look like?   I look like _____.

C **Pair work.** Describe a friend or a family member to a partner. Use the sentences in **A** to help you.

My mom has dark, curly hair and . . .

2 Listening

What does he look like?

 A Emily is at the airport. Listen and check (✓) the correct box.
(CD 1, Track 6)

Emily is looking for her ☐ dad ☐ nephew ☐ uncle.

 B Listen again. Emily is looking for a man. What does he look like?
Circle the correct answers. (CD 1, Track 7)

1. He's tall / short.
2. He's in his 20s / 30s / 40s.

3. He has short / long hair.
4. He has blond / brown hair.

 C Listen again. Who is the man? Check (✓) the correct picture.
What is different about him now? Tell a partner. (CD 1, Track 8)

World Link

The Chinese invented eyeglasses. The explorer Marco Polo saw people in China wearing glasses as early as 1275.

ask**&**
ANSWER
Do you change your hairstyle often? Why or why not?

3 Reading

Celebrity doubles

Do you, a family member, or a friend look like a famous person?

A Read the news article on page 9.

B Read the sentences. Circle *True* or *False*. If a sentence is false, make it true.

1. Andrew Barn looks like a famous movie star.   True   False

2. Andrew Barn is a hairdresser from Manchester, England.   True   False

3. Many celebrity doubles are actually in movies.   True   False

4. The most popular celebrity doubles look like athletes, actors, and world leaders.   True   False

5. Celebrity doubles can make good money.   True   False

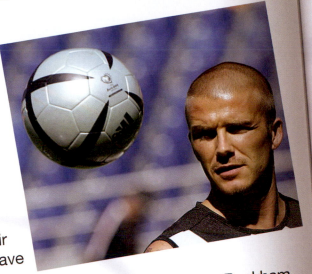

a celebrity = a famous person

Star Talk

Celebrity Doubles

A group of teenagers is standing outside a hair salon in Manchester, England. Many of them have cameras and are looking in the salon window. They want to see soccer player David Beckham. A man in the salon looks like Beckham (he has blond hair and Beckham's good looks). But the man in the salon isn't the famous soccer player. He's Andrew Barn—a twenty-two-year-old hairdresser.

Barn isn't surprised by the teenagers. People often stop him on the street and want to take his picture. Barn is a hairdresser, but he also makes money as a Beckham double. Barn travels all over Europe as David Beckham. Newspapers often take his photo. It's an exciting life for the hairdresser from Manchester.

Today, many companies work with celebrity doubles. The most popular celebrity doubles look like famous athletes, pop singers, and actors. The companies pay doubles to go to parties and business meetings. Doubles are also on TV and in newspaper ads.

Why do people want to look like a celebrity? An Anna Kournikova double in the U.S. says, "I can make good money. I also make a lot of people happy."

ask&
ANSWER

Who are popular celebrities in your country? What are they famous for?
Imagine you can invite a celebrity double to a class party. Who do you want to invite? Why?

Describing people

A Complete the sentences below with the correct form of *be* or *have*. Use the chart to help you.

What does she look like?	
be + adjective/prepositional phrase	*have* + (adjective) noun
Christina is tall and slim. She's in her twenties. She's young.	Mayumi has brown eyes and straight, black hair.

1. Ricardo __has__ curly hair.
2. Monique _____ in her eighties. She _____ elderly.
3. I _____ blue eyes.
4. Max and Charlie are twins. Max _____ a beard and a mustache. Charlie _____ clean-shaven. They both _____ blond hair.
5. Tanya's dad _____ average height.
6. Damon _____ heavy. He weighs about 136 kilos!

B **Pair work.** Look at the pictures of these famous people. Take turns describing each person. Say as much as you can.

Yao Ming   Macy Gray   Luciano Pavarotti   Maria Sharapova

C **Pair work.** Think of a famous person. Describe the person to your partner. Your partner guesses the person.

> This person is a man. He's a famous singer. He's tall. He has black hair and . . .

Guess who?

A Read the paragraph on the right. Then write five or six sentences about a classmate. Don't write your classmate's name.

B **Pair work.** Exchange your writing with a partner. Guess the person.

> My classmate is in his twenties. He's average height—he's about 172 centimeters. He has short, straight, brown hair. He has dark brown eyes (I think). He's clean-shaven, and he wears glasses.

6 Communication

Family photos

 **A** **Pair work.** Look at the photos of famous brothers and sisters. Match a person (1–6) with his or her brother or sister (a–f). Check your answers on page 154.

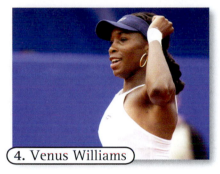  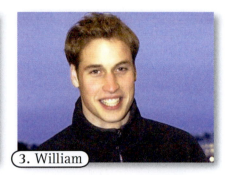

1. Ben Affleck 2. Liv Tyler 3. William

4. Venus Williams 5. Enrique Iglesias 6. Ashley Judd

a. Wynona b. Julio Jr. c. Serena

 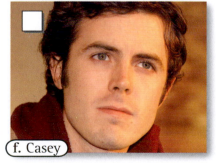

d. Harry e. Mia f. Casey

 B **Pair work.** Look at each famous pair. How are they different? How are they similar?

Check out the World Link video. **Practice your English online at** http://elt.thomson.com/worldlink

2 Express Yourself!

Lesson A | Feelings

---

 1 Vvocabulary Link ⟷

How do they feel?

A **Pair work.** How do these people feel? Match a word in the box with a person in the picture. Take turns telling your partner.

> **Synonyms**
> happy = glad
> angry = mad
> nervous = worried, stressed
> scared = afraid

Feelings

1. ~~happy~~
2. bored
3. angry
4. nervous
5. sad
6. scared
7. embarrassed

> The woman in the red coat is happy.

B Look at the picture again. What are the people doing?
Complete the sentences. Use the correct form of the verbs in the box.

> ~~smile~~   laugh   yell   blush   cry   frown

1. The woman in the red coat _is smiling_.
2. The woman in the blue jeans _____.
3. The child on the bus _____.
4. The businessman _____.
5. The cab driver _____.
6. The driver in front of the cab _____.

C **Pair work.** Give reasons for the feelings of the people in the picture. Tell your partner.

> The women are happy.
> Maybe they're going to the movies.

A Listen to three conversations. Number the pictures 1, 2, or 3 in the order you hear. (CD 1, Track 9)

 B Listen again. How does each speaker feel? Complete the sentences with the correct adjective. (CD 1, Track 10)

1. Angie is nervous / bored. 2. Carolyn is scared / sad. 3. Vicki is happy / angry.

ask**&**
ANSWER

What makes you happy? sad? angry? When you're sad or angry, do you cry? When you are nervous, what do you do?

3 Pronunciation

Linking sounds with 's

 A Listen to the sentences. Notice the pronunciation of the underlined words. (CD 1, Track 11)

1. The <u>man is</u> laughing.   The <u>man's</u> laughing.
2. The <u>bus is</u> coming.   The <u>bus's</u> coming.
3. <u>Why is</u> she frowning?   <u>Why's</u> she frowning?

 B Listen and circle the choices you hear. (CD 1, Track 12)

1. Tina's / Tina is studying in the library.
2. My sister's / sister is nervous. She's / She is studying for a test.
3. When's / When is your class?
4. Cintra's dad's / dad is talking on the phone.
5. How's / How is your family doing?
6. Toshi's car's / car is not working.

 C **Pair work.** Practice saying the sentences in A and B with a partner.

World Link

According to a study of 65 countries in the UK's *New Scientist* magazine, the happiest people in the world live in Nigeria, followed by Mexico, Venezuela, El Salvador, and Puerto Rico

4 Speaking

How's it going?

 A Read the conversation and listen. How is Katy? Explain your answer to a partner. (CD 1, Track 13)

Jim: Hi, Katy.

Katy: Hey, Jim. How's it going?

Jim: Great! How're you doing?

Katy: I'm stressed.

Jim: Yeah? What's wrong?

Katy: Oh, I have an important test tomorrow.

Jim: Well, why aren't you studying?

Katy: I'm kind of tired.

Jim: Come on. Let's have a cup of coffee. Then you can study.

Katy: Okay, sounds good!

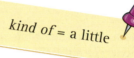
kind of = a little

B **Pair work.** Practice the conversation with a partner. Then ask your partner how he or she is today.

C **Pair work.** Read the two situations below. Write two new conversations on a separate sheet of paper. Use the conversation in A and the Useful Expressions to help you.

Situation 1	Situation 2
Student A: You're mad. You have two tickets to a basketball game tonight. You're going with your friend, but your friend is late.	**Student A:** You're unhappy. You live in New York. Your cousin lives in Boston. She wants you to visit her. You're afraid of flying on a plane.
Student B: Your suggestion: Take a taxi to the game. Maybe the friend is there.	**Student B:** Your suggestion: rent a car and drive from New York to Boston together.

Useful Expressions:			
Asking how someone is			
How's it going?	Great!	How're you doing?	(I'm) Fine.
	Fine.		OK.
	OK. / All right.		So-so.
	So-so.		I'm stressed.
	Not so good.		I'm tired.
	Don't ask!		I'm worried.

 D **Group work.** Role-play one conversation for another pair.

5 Language Link

Review of the present continuous

> Use the present continuous for actions happening now.
>
> subject + *am* / *is* / *are* + verb *-ing*

 A **Pair work.** Imagine you are looking out your apartment window. What are your neighbors doing? Write three sentences about each apartment. Use the present continuous.

1. In apartment B, a man and woman are watching TV.
2. _____
3. _____
4. _____
5. _____
6. _____
7. _____
8. _____
9. _____

 B **Pair work.** Think of questions to ask about the picture. Take turns asking and answering the questions with a partner.

1. _____
2. _____
3. _____
4. _____
5. _____
6. _____

> In apartment A, why are the people laughing?

> Maybe they're watching a funny TV show.

 A **Pair work**. Look at the picture above with your partner and answer the questions.

- Where are these people?
- How old are they?
- What are they doing?
- How do they feel?

 B **Pair work. Role play.** Choose one of the pairs in the picture. What are they talking about? Role-play a conversation with eight to ten sentences. In your role play, ask for this information:

- How is your partner doing?
- Where is your partner living now?
- What is your partner doing these days?
- Your question: _____
- Your question: _____

Hi, Pilar! It's great to see you! How's it going?

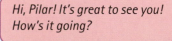

Great! How are you doing?

 C **Group work. Role play.** Perform your role play for another pair.

ask**&**
ANSWER

Do you ever see your classmates from high school?
What are they doing these days?

Express Yourself!

Lesson B | Body language and gestures

Gestures

A What do these gestures mean?
Some sentences are used more than once.

a. Hello! *or* Goodbye!
b. Come here.
c. Look!
d. I don't know.
e. I'm joking.
f. Good luck!

1. point

3. shrug

2. shake hands

4. bow

5. wink

6. wave

7. kiss

8. cross one's fingers

9. call someone

B **Pair work.** Discuss these questions with a partner.

1. Do the gestures in A have the same meaning in your country?
2. Are any of the gestures in A uncommon or rude in your country?
3. Do you know gestures for these expressions?:
   I can't hear you.   Are you talking to me?   You're crazy.   Come here!

2 Listening

What are they doing?

 A Listen to the four conversations. What gestures are the people using in each? Complete the sentences with the correct answer. (CD 1, Track 14)

1. The woman is winking at / waving to her friend.
2. The two women are crossing their fingers / shaking hands.
3. The man is pointing at Anne / crossing his fingers.
4. The man is shrugging / winking.

 B Listen again. Complete each sentence with the correct answer. (CD 1, Track 15)

1. The woman has Connie's wallet / backpack.
2. Jen is embarrassed / nervous about meeting her boyfriend's mom.
3. Anne is starting a new job / studying for a test today.
4. The man and woman are going to a friend's house / theater.

3 Reading

World Greetings

A greeting is a way of saying "hello" to someone. When people greet each other they usually say and do something. What kinds of greetings do you know?

A Read the information.

WorldView World Greetings

 Brazil

Men often shake hands when they meet for the first time. When women meet, they kiss each other on the cheek. Women also kiss male friends to say hello.

When you shake hands, look at the person in the eyes. This shows interest and friendliness.

 New Zealand

Usually, both men and women shake hands when they meet someone for the first time.

Fun fact: *If you see two people pressing their noses together, they are probably Maori. The Maori are the native people of New Zealand. This is their traditional greeting.*

 Japan

When people meet for the first time, they usually bow. In business, people also shake hands.

In formal situations, people often exchange business cards. When you give a business card, give it with two hands. This is polite.

Special note: *In Japan, a smile can have different meanings. It usually means that the person is happy, or that the person thinks something is funny. But it can also mean that the person is embarrassed.*

B Complete the sentences about each picture. Use the information from the reading.

1. In New Zealand, both men and women _____ when they meet for the first time.

2. In _____, people usually _____ when they meet for the first time.

3. This is the traditional greeting for the _____ people of New Zealand.

4. In _____, women often _____ when they meet.

5. In Brazil, look at people _____ when you shake hands.

6. In _____, people smile when they are happy, or sometimes when they are _____.

ask**&**
ANSWER

Are the customs in the reading different or similar in your country? Explain.

With *it*:
Your hat is nice. I like it.

A Study the chart.

Subject	Verb	Object	Subject	Verb	Object pronouns
I You He She We You *(pl.)* They	know(s)	Mary's parents	They	like	me. you. him. her. us. you. them.

B Read the sentences. Circle the subject. Underline the object.

1. (Angie) is hugging her son.
2. Tom is smiling at Jane.
3. Carlos is worried about the test.
4. Do your parents like Indian food?

5. Peter and Cindy are talking to Bill and Anna.
6. Rick and I can meet you and Mike at 3:00.
7. Hiroshi is living with Taylor and me for a month.
8. Maya is calling Beth on her cell phone.

C Rewrite the sentences in **B**. Use the correct subject and object pronouns.

1. _She's hugging him._
2. _____
3. _____
4. _____
5. _____
6. _____
7. _____
8. _____

World Link

Showing the soles of your shoes when sitting is rude in many countries, including Nigeria, Russia, Egypt, and Thailand.

D Read the sentences. Underline and correct the mistakes.

1. Who's that man over there? I think he is winking at I.
   That's my dad. He's not winking at you. He's smiling at we.
2. Bill and me are going to the movies.
   Do you want to come with us?
3. Maria's parents live in Puebla. She calls they every Monday.
   They talk for one hour.
4. Gina is my roommate. I like she a lot.
5. Please don't lie to I. Tell me the truth!

5 Writing

Smiling in e-mail

 A Look at these informal ways of showing meaning in e-mail. Can you add other ideas to the list?

	Example	Meaning
smileys	:-)	I'm happy. / I'm smiling.
	:-D	I'm laughing.
	;-)	I'm joking. I'm winking.
	:-0	I'm surprised.
abbreviations	LOL	laughing out loud
	FYI	for your information

B **Pair work.** Read the e-mail. Then, on a separate piece of paper, write an e-mail to your partner. Tell him or her about something you're doing now. Use the smileys and abbreviations in **A** in the message.

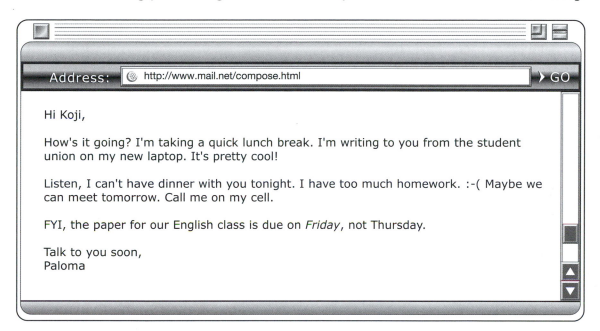

Address: http://www.mail.net/compose.html   ❯ GO

Hi Koji,

How's it going? I'm taking a quick lunch break. I'm writing to you from the student union on my new laptop. It's pretty cool!

Listen, I can't have dinner with you tonight. I have too much homework. :-(Maybe we can meet tomorrow. Call me on my cell.

FYI, the paper for our English class is due on *Friday*, not Thursday.

Talk to you soon,
Paloma

6 Communication

Pantomime

Group work. Get into a group of three people. Read the directions to play this game.

Student A: Choose a sentence below. Act out the sentences for Students B and Students C. Do *not* use words.

Students B and C: Watch Student A. Be the first to say the sentence Student A is doing. If you guess correctly, you get a point. Play until all sentences are done.

I'm hungry.	Relax!	Look at that!	I'm nervous.
This is delicious.	Good luck!	Come here!	This tastes terrible.
Stop it!	Really? That's suprising!	I'm bored.	I'm not listening!
Let's go!	Go away!	I'm angry.	Sit down.
Be quiet.	Peace.	What? I can't hear you.	See you.
I'm sad.	You have a phone call.	He's crazy.	I'm not sure.

 Check out the World Link video.   **Practice your English online at http://elt.thomson.com/worldlink**

What Do We Need?

Lesson A | At the supermarket

1 Vocabulary Link

At the supermarket

A **Pair work.** With a partner, find each of the 20 items below in the picture above and circle them.

Meat and Poultry	Seafood	Produce		Dairy	Drinks
		Vegetables	Fruit		
1. ham	4. fish	6. lettuce	11. apples	15. cheese	19. juice
2. beef	5. shrimp	7. potatoes	12. oranges	16. yogurt	20. soda
3. chicken		8. carrots	13. bananas	17. milk	
		9. corn	14. grapes	18. eggs	
		10. tomatoes			

B **Pair work.** Add other foods and drinks to the list. Share your ideas with the class.

ask&
ANSWER

Which foods are your favorites? Are there any foods you dislike? Why?

Where do you usually buy your food? Is your market similar to the one in the picture? Explain.

2 Listening

Shopping list

  A Listen. Which shopping bag is Allison's? Circle it. (CD 1, Track 16)

ice cream

  B Listen again. Allison's mom changes one item on the list. Put an X on the item in the shopping bag. Write the name of the new item. (CD 1, Track 17)

In unstressed syllables, the vowel sound is reduced. The schwa /ə/ is the symbol for these vowels.

3 Pronunciation

Weak vowel sounds

  A Listen to the words. Notice the stressed syllables in blue and the unstressed vowels (/ə/). (CD 1, Track 18)

ba**na**na = bənanə   **car**rot = carrət   **ket**chup = ketchəp

  B Listen and say the words. Put a line [\ ] through the unstressed, reduced vowels. (CD 1, Track 19)

chicken	vanilla	vitamin	hamburger
soda	potato	lettuce	paper
orange	bandage	sugar	pizza

World Link

There are over 7,000 varieties of rice, divided into three main groups—long, medium, and short grain. Rice is the chief food for more than half the world's population.

4 Speaking

We need potatoes.

 A Read the conversation and listen. Underline the foods Ken and Rachel have. Circle the foods they need. (CD 1, Track 20)

Ken:	Rachel, I'm making a shopping list for tomorrow's barbecue. We have chicken. What else do we need?
Rachel:	Let's see . . . we need some potatoes. Buy five pounds.
Ken:	Okay, five pounds of potatoes.
Rachel:	We also need lettuce and tomatoes for the salad.
Ken:	And what about drinks? Do we need any?
Rachel:	No, we don't. We have soda and juice.
Ken:	Okay. I'm going to the store. See you in a bit.

In the U.S., pounds (lbs.) are used.
1 pound = .45 kg

 B **Pair work.** Practice the conversation with your partner.

 C **Pair work.** Look at the shopping list.

- What other things do you need for a barbecue? Add them to the shopping list.
- Use the items on the list and the Useful Expressions to make a conversation like the one in A.

Shopping list: Saturday barbecue	Useful Expressions:
(X = items you have now)	Expressing need
X two chickens	**Do we need any** drinks?
X juice	• Yes, we do.
X soda	• Yes, we need some.
_____	• No, we don't.
_____	• No, we don't need any.
_____	**We need** twelve hot dogs.
_____	**We need (some)** hamburger. Buy five pounds.

 D **Pair work.** Imagine that you are having a class party. Talk about the things you need.

 E **Group work.** Compare your list with another pair's. Together, make one list.

We need food for the party. Let's have pizza and . . .

Count/Noncount nouns with *some* and *any*

(A) **Pair work.** Read the sentences. Look at the underlined words. Which are count nouns? Which are noncount nouns? Tell your partner.

> **Noncount nouns**
> • don't have *a*, *an*, or a number in front of the noun
> • are always singular

1. Let's make a smoothie. We need <u>yogurt</u>, <u>sugar</u>, <u>ice</u>, and two <u>bananas</u>.
2. Are you thirsty? There's <u>water</u> in the refrigerator.
3. I cut my finger. Do you have a <u>bandage</u>?

(B) Complete the sentences with *a*, *an*, or nothing.

1. Do you want _____ magazine to read?
2. Do you want _____ rice or _____ baked potato with your meal?
3. Please use _____ soap to wash your hands and face.
4. There's _____ toothpaste in the bathroom to brush your teeth.
5. Billy wants _____ fruit with his lunch. Give him _____ apple.
6. Is there _____ salt in this soup?
7. Let's get _____ cake for the class party.
8. Sophie wants _____ soda, and Mrs. Allen wants _____ tea.

> With many noncount nouns, we use measure words. These make the item countable.
>
> **a cup of** coffee
> **a bottle of** water
> **a can of** soda
> **a glass of** milk/water/juice
> **a piece of** bread/meat
> **a bar of** soap

(C) Study the chart. Then complete the conversation with *some* or *any*.

	Question	Positive answer	Negative answer
Noncount nouns	Do we have **any** lettuce?	Yes, we have **some** (lettuce).	No, we **don't have any** (lettuce).
Plural count nouns	Do we have **any** potatoes?	Yes, we have **some** (potatoes). Yes, we have **three** (potatoes).	No, we **don't have any** (potatoes).

Andrew: Great party, Liz!

Liz: Thanks! Do you want (1) _Some_ coffee?

Andrew: No, thanks. I have (2) _some_. Listen, do you need (3) _any_ help with dinner?

Liz: Actually, yes. Can you make the salad?

Andrew: Sure! But first, do you have (4) _any_ soap?

Liz: For the salad?!

Andrew: No, I want to wash my hands.

Liz: Yeah, there's (5) _any_ next to the sink.

Andrew: Thanks. Now, let's see . . . do you have (6) _any_ lettuce?

Liz: Yes, there's (7) _Some_ in the refrigerator.

Andrew: Great. Is there (8) _any_ yogurt for the dressing?

Liz: No, I don't have (9) _any_.

Andrew: OK. I'll go to the store and buy (10) _Some_ now.

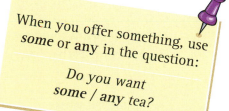

> When you offer something, use *some* or *any* in the question:
>
> Do you want
> *some / any* tea?

(D) **Pair work.** Practice the conversation with your partner.

Island Survivor!

 Read about this TV show. Then answer the questions.

There is a new reality show on TV. On this show, people stay on an island for one month to win money. Here is some information about the island:

- It is in the Pacific Ocean.
- In the afternoon, it is very hot—100 degrees F / 38 degrees C.
- There's very little drinking water on the island.
- There are some fruit trees on the island.

You want to be on this TV show. For your stay on the island, you can choose six items from the list below. Is there anything you want to add to the list? Write it. Then circle the six items you need.

meat	toothpaste	bananas	bandages	knife
bottled water	soap	oranges	coffee or tea	matches
rice	sunscreen	magazines	toilet paper	_____
bread	hat	shampoo	vitamins	_____

 Group work. Join a group of three to four people. Compare your answers. **Explain your choices. Together make** *one* **list of six items.**

C **Group work. Explain your final list to the class.**

> We need some bottled water. There's very little drinking water on the island.

What Do We Need?

1 Vyocabulary Link

At the mall

A Look at the stores in this shopping mall. Match a name with a store.

Stores

a. department store

b. music store

c. bookstore

d. drugstore

e. electronics store

f. stationery store

g. toy store

B **Pair work.** Look at the shopping list. Which store sells each of these things? Tell your partner.

> a sweater
>
> an English-German dictionary
>
> a new coffee maker
>
> a DVD player
>
> Dance the Night Away CD
>
> bandages
>
> a birthday card
>
> a doll

> A department store sells sweaters.

World Link

A *shopaholic* is someone who is addicted to shopping. Studies suggest that 1 in 20 Americans is a shopaholic.

C **Pair work.** What other things can you buy in the stores in A? Tell your partner.

ask & ANSWER

Is there a mall in your city? Where is it? What stores are there in the mall? What's a good place to buy clothing? music? computers?

2 Listening

Flea markets

 A Listen to this TV show. Number the photos 1–3 in the order you hear them. (CD 1, Track 21)

The Chatuchak Weekend Market, Bangkok

The Maxwell Street Market, Chicago

The Paris Flea Market,

 B Listen again. What can you buy at each market? Check (✓) the items. (CD 1, Track 22)

	traditional art	furniture	traditional jewelry	new and used clothing	international foods	traditional clothing
Paris	☐	☐	☐	☐	☐	☐
Maxwell	☐	☐	☐	☐	☐	☐
Chatuchak	☐	☐	☐	☐	☐	☐

ask & ANSWER

Which flea market is interesting to you? Why? Is there a flea market or large marketplace in your city? Where is it? What can you buy there?

3 Reading

Garage Sale Bargains

What do you think a garage sale is?

A Read the article on page 29. Then complete these sentences.

1. At a garage sale, people usually sell _____ items
   a. new   b. used

2. A person has a garage sale _____.
   a. in a store   b. in front of his or her house

3. People usually go to garage sales on _____.
   a. Saturday and Sunday   b. Monday and Tuesday

Shop Here Now

Garage Sale Bargains

Do you need a sofa or an interesting piece of art? If you don't have a lot of money, try a garage sale! Every weekend, in cities around Canada and the United States,
5 people sell unwanted things in front of their houses—old books, used clothes and jewelry, videos and CDs, old furniture, and much more!

Patricia Evans lives in Detroit, Michigan. She goes to garage sales on the weekends.
10 "On Friday nights, I look on the Web for the best garage sales in my city," she says. "I make a list. Then on Saturday and Sunday I go from sale to sale."

And what does she find? "There's a lot of junk at some garage sales—you know, used clothes and kids' toys. But sometimes, you can find something really interesting—for a great price! I have some beautiful antiques. One is a small table from the 1920s. The price? Five dollars! I also have an
15 old radio from the 1940s. It was free. It doesn't work, but I like to fix things."

Patricia doesn't only buy antiques at garage sales. "Here's a set of Yu-Gi-Oh trading cards for my nine-year-old nephew. In a store, this set costs $12. At the garage sale, it was $1. That's cheap!"

B **Find these words in the reading.**

1. This word in line 12 means *something old or not useful*: _____

2. This word in line 14 means *old things—furniture, jewelry, or other items—that are worth money*: _____

3. This word in line 17 means *not expensive*: _____

ask **&**
ANSWER

What do you do with your old clothes, furniture, books, bikes, or TVs?
Check (✓) the sentence.
Explain your answer.

☐ I sell my old things.

☐ I give my old things to someone.

☐ I put my old things in the garbage.

☐ other _____

Do you ever buy used clothes, furniture, CDs, or videos? Where do you buy these things?

4 Language Link

Some/any; much/many; a lot of

A **Pair work.** With a partner, look at the picture below and complete the sentences in the chart. Use the words in the box.

~~shoes~~   clothing   furniture   toys   hats

	Noncount nouns			Count nouns		
Positive	There's	a lot of	*clothing*	There are	a lot of	*shoes* .
		some	jewelry.		some	*hats* .
Negative	There isn't	much	*furniture*.	There aren't	many	books.
		any	software.		any	*toys* .

B Complete the sentences with *some, any, much, many,* or *a lot of.*

1. John won $1,000,000 in the lottery! Now he has _____*a lot of*_____ money.

2. Barry only has $5 in his bank account. He doesn't have _____*any*_____ money.

3. Rita has _____*some*_____ beautiful jade jewelry: two bracelets and a pair of earrings.

4. Carla is an only child. She doesn't have _____*any*_____ brothers or sisters.

5. Leo is really popular. He has _____*many*_____ friends.

6. I don't have _____*many*_____ friends—just two from college. But, we're very close.

5 Writing

My favorite place to shop

 A Read about this person's favorite place to shop. Then write five or six sentences about your favorite place to shop.

- What's the name of the place?
- What kind of store is it?
- What can you buy there?
- Where is it?
- Why do you like it?

My favorite place to shop is Amoeba Music. It's on Sunset Boulevard in Hollywood. This store sells new and used records, CDs, DVDs, and videos. Amoeba sells all kinds of music—pop, classical, rock, jazz, dance, hip-hop. You can find some good movies and a lot of great music at a great price!

 B **Pair work.** Exchange your writing with a partner. Ask your partner one question about his or her favorite place.

6 Communication

Shopping spree

 A **Pair work.** Read about Jessie. Then describe her apartment with a partner.

Jessie is 22-year-old university exchange student. She's living in your country for one year. She lives in a small apartment near her school. This is her apartment.

 There isn't much furniture in the apartment.

B **Pair work.** Jessie's parents live in the United States. They want to visit her. Help Jessie prepare for her parents' visit.

- What does her apartment need? Make a list.
- Where can she buy the things? Put your ideas on the list.

Things Jessie needs	Place to shop
chairs	Lotte Department Store

She needs some chairs in the kitchen. She can buy them at Lotte Department Store.

C **Group work.** Compare your list with another pair.

  Check out the World Link video. **Practice your English online at** http://elt.thomson.com/worldlink

1 Storyboard

 Pair work. Rieko and Eva are roommates. Look at the pictures and work with a partner to complete the conversations. More than one answer is possible for most blanks.

1 — Hey Rieko, _____ _____?
I'm going to the supermarket.

2 — Can I go with you? I need some _____.
Sure! Let's go.

Near the supermarket . . .
Let's go into that _____ store. I need _____.
OK.

Later, at the market . . .
4 — Do we _____ _____?
No, we have some at home.

5 — Do we need _____?
Yeah. Let's get _____.

6 — I think we have everything. Let's _____.

 Pair work. Practice the conversation with a partner. Then change roles and practice again.

Pair work. Describe a person in the picture below to your partner. Don't say the person's name. Your partner guesses the person.

 Pair work. Talk about the picture.

This person is tall. The person has long hair and . . .

- Where are these people?
- What are they doing?
- Which people are meeting for the first time? How do you know?
- Ask one question about the picture.

 Pair work. Role play. Choose one pair or group of people. With a partner, role-play a conversation of five to six sentences between the people.

Hi, I'm Felipe . . .

Hi, Felipe. My name is . . .

3 Odd word out

 A Look at the words. Circle the one that is different in each group.

1. chicken	beef	potato	ham
2. nervous	embarrassed	angry	happy
3. grape	carrot	corn	lettuce
4. blond	gray	curly	black
5. cheese	yogurt	milk	orange juice
6. heavyset	short	slim	thin
7. bored	wink	wave	shrug
8. shampoo	TV	toothpaste	soap

 B **Pair work**. Compare and explain your answers with a partner.

> *For number 1, potato is different. A potato is a vegetable. Chicken, beef, and ham are meat.*

4 Do you ever . . . ?

 A Read each question. Answer *Yes* or *No*. Then write a sentence to give some extra information. In your answer, use the correct pronouns for the underlined words.

1. Do <u>you</u> ever give <u>your mom</u> flowers?

   <u>Yes. I give her flowers on her birthday.</u>

2. Do <u>you</u> ever speak to <u>your dad</u> in English?

   _____

3. Do <u>you</u> ever take <u>the bus</u> to school?

   _____

4. Do <u>you</u> ever write letters to <u>your friends</u>?

   _____

5. Does <u>your teacher</u> ever give <u>the class</u> homework?

   _____

6. Do <u>your friends</u> ever make <u>you</u> angry?

   _____

B **Pair work**. Ask your partner the questions in **A**. Listen to his or her answers. Then, ask your partner one more question.

> *Do you ever speak in English to your dad?*

> *No. I always speak to him in Spanish.*

> *Does he understand English?*

> *No. Not really.*

5 Listening: The perfect diet?

 A Tino and Mary are talking about Tino's diet. Listen. Which foods can Tino eat? Check (✓) them. Which can't he eat? Mark them with an X. (CD 1, Track 23)

 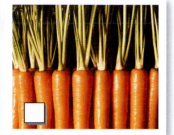  

 B Listen again. Circle *True* or *False*. If the sentence is false, make it true. (CD 1, Track 24)

1. Tino can't eat any vegetables.	True	False
2. Tino eats a lot of sugar.	True	False
3. Tino takes vitamins.	True	False
4. Mary isn't worried about Tino's diet.	True	False

C **Pair work.** Discuss this question with a partner and explain your opinion: Is Tino's diet healthy?

6 Talk about . . .

 A **Group work.** Get into a group of three people and do this activity.

1. One person chooses a topic from the list and says it to the group.
2. Each person in the group asks the first person a question about the topic. That person answers each question.
3. Take turns and repeat steps 1 and 2 for each topic.

- your hobbies
- why you are learning English
- your favorite music
- a country you want to visit
- your favorite TV show
- your favorite food
- your best friend
- something you don't like

1 Vocabulary Link

In the neighborhood

A Min Chul is a new student at a university in the U.S. Below are some places in his neighborhood. Match each word in the box with a photo.

1. bank
2. gym
3. movie theater
4. Internet café
5. laundromat
6. post office
7. library
8. hair salon

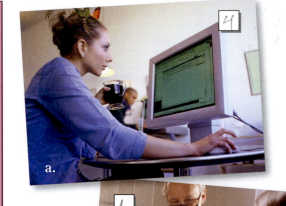

a.

b.

c.

d.

e.

f.

g.

h.

B **Pair work.** What things can you do at each place in A? Make a list and then share your ideas with the class.

You can check your e-mail at the Internet café.

2 Listening

Where are they?

 A Listen to four conversations. Number the pictures as you listen. **(CD 1, Track 25)**

 a

 b

 c

 d

☐ to change money
☐ to get money

☐ to buy stamps
☐ to mail a letter

☐ to cut her hair
☐ to color her hair

☐ to have coffee
☐ to check e-mail

 B Listen again. Why is each person at the place? Check (✓) the correct answer. **(CD 1, Track 26)**

3 Pronunciation

Sentence stress

 A Listen to the sentences. Notice how the most important words are *stressed* (said louder). **(CD 1, Track 27)**

1. A: Where's the **post office**?
   B: It's in the **middle** of the **block**.

2. A: Where's the **bus stop**?
   B: It's on the **corner** of **Fourth** and **Main Streets**.

 B Listen to the conversations. Underline the words that are stressed. **(CD 1, Track 28)**

1. A: Where's Terry?
   B: She's in front of the theater.

2. A: Where's the car parked?
   B: It's next to a gym on Eighth Avenue.

3. A: Is there a laundromat near here?
   B: Yes, it's across from the café on Fourteenth Street.

 C **Pair work.** Practice the conversations in **A** and **B** with a partner. Pay attention to stress.

World Link

Americans say *laundromat*, but in British English it's called a *laundrette*. Some words are also spelled differently in American and British English, e.g., *theater* (American) and *theatre* (British).

4 Speaking

Is there a theater near here?

A Min Chul and Paulo are classmates. Listen to their conversation. What are they looking for? Where is it? (CD 1, Track 29)

Paulo:	Hey, Min Chul. I think we're lost. Where's the theater?
Min Chul:	I'm not sure. I think it's on Albany Avenue.
Paulo:	Hmmm . . . I don't see it. Let's ask someone.
Min Chul:	Okay. Excuse me.

Woman:	Yes?
Min Chul:	Is there a movie theater near here?
Woman:	Yes, there's one on the corner of Bloor Street West and Albany Avenue.
Min Chul:	Thanks a lot!

B Group work. Practice the conversation in groups of three.

C Pair work. With a partner, take turns asking and answering about the places on the map below. Use the Useful Expressions to help you.

Partner A asks about:

Bradfort Park	a store
a laundromat	a post office
a school	a deli

Partner B asks about:

City Hall	a bank
an Internet café	a parking lot
a church	a hotel

Useful Expressions: Asking for and giving directions	
To ask about a specific place	Excuse me. Where's the Bridge Theater? It's on Albany Avenue. It's on the corner of Bloor Street West and Albany Avenue.
To ask about a place in general	Is there a movie theater near here? Yes, there's one on Albany Avenue. No, there isn't. Sorry, I don't know.

5 Language Link

Prepositions of place

 A Look at the map and read the e-mail. Pay attention to the words in bold.

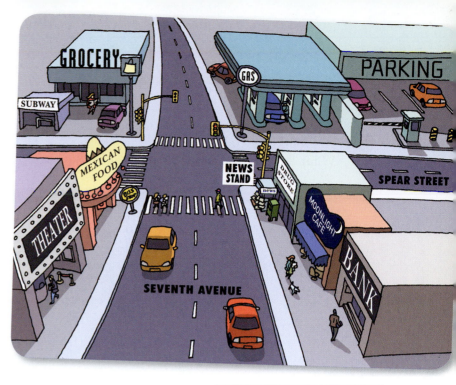

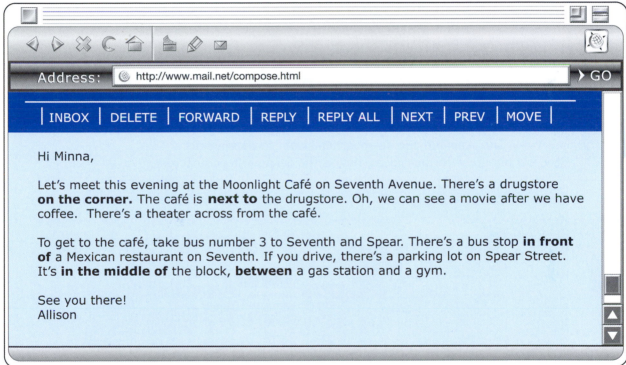

Address: http://www.mail.net/compose.html **>GO**

| INBOX | DELETE | FORWARD | REPLY | REPLY ALL | NEXT | PREV | MOVE |

Hi Minna,

Let's meet this evening at the Moonlight Café on Seventh Avenue. There's a drugstore **on the corner.** The café is **next to** the drugstore. Oh, we can see a movie after we have coffee. There's a theater across from the café.

To get to the café, take bus number 3 to Seventh and Spear. There's a bus stop **in front of** a Mexican restaurant on Seventh. If you drive, there's a parking lot on Spear Street. It's **in the middle of** the block, **between** a gas station and a gym.

See you there!
Allison

B Look again at the map. Complete the sentences with the words in bold in A.

1. There's a mailbox _____ Seventh Avenue. It's _____ a newsstand.
2. The grocery store is _____ of Seventh and Spear. It's _____ a gas station.
3. There's a subway station _____ the grocery store.
4. The café is _____ the block. It's _____ the drugstore and the bank.

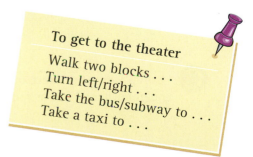

To get to the theater

Walk two blocks . . .
Turn left/right . . .
Take the bus/subway to . . .
Take a taxi to . . .

C **Pair work.** Think of a place to meet your partner. Give him or her directions to the place from your school. Use the example in A to help you.

Pair work. Look at the neighborhood below and describe it. What places are there? Where are they? What are the problems with this neighborhood?

Many of the buildings are old.

 Pair work. The people of the neighborhood want to improve it. Here is a picture with their ideas. How is the neighborhood different?

There are a lot of trees on the street now. It's much nicer!

 Group work. Are there other ways to improve this neighborhood? Share your ideas with another pair.

ask & ANSWER

Which are the best neighborhoods or areas in your city? Describe one to a partner.

Around the World

1 Vocabulary Link

Two cities

$$$ expensive
$$ affordable
$ cheap

 A Study the information about these two cities.

	Los Angeles	Juneau, Alaska
cost of living (for housing, clothing, food)	$$$	$$
population	3,700,000 people	31,000
weather	85°F / 29°C in summer 40°F / 4°C in winter	50°F / 10°C 32°F / 0°C
transportation		
crime		
traffic		
pollution		

B **Pair work.** Complete the chart below. Then tell your partner which city is better to live in and why.

	Los Angeles	Juneau
1. expensive	☐	☐
2. a lot of people	☐	☐
3. cold in winter	☐	☐

	Los Angeles	Juneau
4. has public transportation	☐	☐
5. more crime	☐	☐
6. a lot of traffic	☐	☐
7. very little pollution	☐	☐

ask & ANSWER

What's the best thing about your hometown? What's the worst?

2 Listening

In the suburbs

A Toshi and Isabel are studying English in London. Listen. Circle the correct city. (CD 1, Track 30)

1. Isabel lives in Madrid / Getafe.

2. She goes to school in Madrid / Getafe.

B Listen again. Which words describe the city Isabel lives in? Check (✓) the words. (CD 1, Track 31)

- ☐ big city
- ☐ small city
- ☐ a lot of fun
- ☐ not very exciting
- ☐ affordable
- ☐ expensive

ask & ANSWER

What are good reasons to live in a suburb?
What is good about living in a big city?

3 Reading

The best cities to live in

World Link

La Paz, Bolivia, at 4 km above sea level, is the world's highest capital. Because there is less oxygen at this altitude, La Paz has very few natural fires.

What do you think are the best cities in the world? Why are they the best?

A Read the travel articles about the best cities to live in on page 43.

B Read the sentences. Which city does each sentence describe? Sometimes both cities are possible.

	Hong Kong	San Jose
1. Housing isn't expensive here.	☐	☐
2. This city is famous for its food.	☐	☐
3. The weather here is good all year.	☐	☐
4. Air pollution is a problem here.	☐	☐
5. There are parks and other beautiful places outside the city.	☐	☐
6. This city was once a fishing village.	☐	☐

ask & ANSWER

Do you want to live in the cities in the reading? Why or why not?
What is important to you in a place to live? Put these items in order from 1 (very important) to 4 (not so important). Explain your reasons.

___ weather   ___ safety   ___ cost of living   ___ nightlife

The *Best Cities* to Live in

SAN JOSE, COSTA RICA

When people think of Costa Rica, they imagine rain forests, rivers, and beautiful beaches. These things are not in San Jose. But this city is still one of the world's best. Why?

Unlike other cities in Central and South America, San Jose has comfortable weather all year (15°C/60°F to 26°C/79°F).

Housing is affordable in San Jose. Also, many of the city's older neighborhoods are very beautiful and have small hotels, art galleries, and cafés.

Beautiful volcanoes and mountains surround the city. You can visit them easily from San Jose.

Minuses: There's good public transportation, but traffic and air pollution are a problem in the city center.

The Best Cities to Live in

HONG KONG, CHINA

Why live in Hong Kong? Here are two good reasons.

The city: This lively city—once a small fishing village—is today an international business center. It is an interesting mix of East and West, old and new. Modern skyscrapers are next to small temples. Popular nightclubs are close to traditional teahouses. Busy crowds fill the streets at all hours of the day. But outside the city, there are parks for walking or relaxing.

The food: Hong Kong is famous for its wonderful native dishes (try the dim sum). There's also food from Europe, North America, and other parts of Asia.

Minuses: This small city has a large population. How many people live in Hong Kong? Almost seven million! That's why housing is often very expensive. Traffic and air pollution are also a problem.

4 Language Link

How much/How many

 A Study the chart. Then circle the correct word to complete each sentence below.

How many parks are there in your city?	How much pollution is there in your city?
There are **a lot** (of parks).	There's **a lot** (of pollution).
There are **some**.	There's **some**.
There are **two**.	There's **a little**. / There **isn't much**.
There **aren't many**.	There **isn't any**. / There's **none**.
There **aren't any**. / There are **none**.	

1. Use *how many* with count / noncount nouns.
2. Use *how much* with count / noncount nouns.

 B **Pair work.** **Look at the chart. Complete the questions below with** *How much* **or** *How many*. **Then take turns asking and answering the questions.**

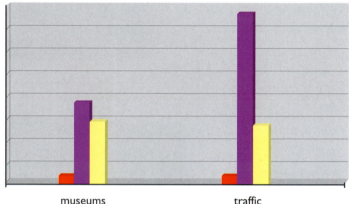

museums   traffic

1. _____ museums are there in Auckland?   There are ___ some ___.
2. _____ traffic is there in Corozal?   There isn't _____.
3. _____ museums are there in Bangkok?   There are _____.
4. _____ traffic is there in Bangkok?   There is _____.
5. _____ museums are there in Corozal?   There aren't _____.

C **Write four questions about your city on a separate piece of paper. Use** *How much* **or** *How many*.

Student A ask about: nightclubs, traffic, crime, stores open 24 hours

Student B ask about: shopping malls, pollution, people from other countries, beaches

 D **Pair work.** **Take turns asking and answering the question in C with a partner.**

5 Writing

My city

 A Read about Ahmed's city. Then write about a city you know. Use the questions to help you write.

- Where do you live—in a big city or a suburb?
- What is your city famous for?
- What are some of the city's problems?

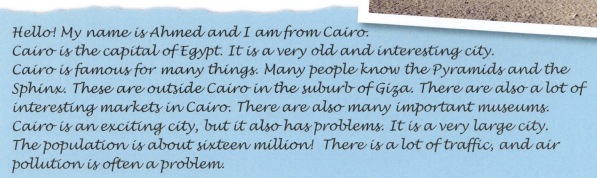

Hello! My name is Ahmed and I am from Cairo.
Cairo is the capital of Egypt. It is a very old and interesting city.
Cairo is famous for many things. Many people know the Pyramids and the Sphinx. These are outside Cairo in the suburb of Giza. There are also a lot of interesting markets in Cairo. There are also many important museums.
Cairo is an exciting city, but it also has problems. It is a very large city. The population is about sixteen million! There is a lot of traffic, and air pollution is often a problem.

 B **Pair work.** Share your writing with a partner. Did your partner answer the questions in A?

6 Communication

Hosting the World Cup

Every four years, the World Cup is in a different country. Many countries compete to host the games. Imagine that your country wants to host a future World Cup.

 A **Pair work.** Discuss these questions with a partner. Use the ideas below to help you. Write your notes on a separate piece of paper.

- Why is your country a good place to host the World Cup?
- What things does it have?
- What problems are there?

sports stadiums	good hotels	airports and train stations
good weather	good restaurants	pollution
public transportation	interesting things to do	traffic	other _____

 B **Group work.** Get together with another pair and compare your answers. Do you think your country could be chosen to host the World Cup?

 Check out the World Link video. **Practice your English online at http://elt.thomson.com/worldlink**

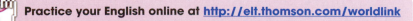

1 Vocabulary Link

How's the weather?

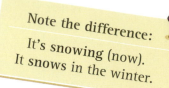
Note the difference:
It's snowing (now).
It snows in the winter.

A **Pair work.** Look at the weather report. Match a word in the box with a city. Then, tell your partner about each city.

Adjectives

a. sunny

b. cloudy

c. windy

d. clear

Verbs

e. raining

f. snowing

Address: http://www.weathertoday.net/today.html   ▶ GO

HOME | MY PAGE | AROUND THE GLOBE | NEWS | STORE

TODAY'S WEATHER

Around the globe

Montreal, Canada
28°F/-2°C
1. It's _snowing_.

Portland, Oregon, USA
55°F/13°C
2. It's _windy_.

Shanghai, China
42°F/5.5°C
3. It's _clear_.

Buenos Aires, Argentina
90°F/32°C
4. It's _sunny_ and _clear_.

Suva, Fiji
70°F/21°C
5. It's _raining_.

B What's the temperature in each city in **A**? Use the words in the box to talk about each city.

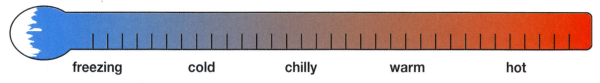

freezing   cold   chilly   warm   hot

It's hot in Buenos Aires in summer.

ask & ANSWER

Do you like hot weather? Do you like cold weather? Why or why not?
In your city, what's the weather like in the summer? winter? spring? autumn?

2 Listening

It's hot outside.

 A Listen to the three conversations. How's the weather? Check (✓) the correct pictures. (CD 1, Track 32)

1.   2.   3.

Wmdy

W

Sunny

 B Listen again. Do the people go outside or stay inside? Check (✓) the boxes. (CD 1, Track 33)

	go outside	stay inside
1.	☐	☐
2.	☐	☐
3.	☐	☐

3 Pronunciation

Should and *shouldn't*

 A Listen to these sentences. Notice the pronunciation of *should* and *shouldn't*. (CD 1, Track 34)

We **should** drive. It's raining.

We **shouldn't** drive. It's sunny.

 B Listen. Circle the word you hear. (CD 1, Track 35)

1. You should / shouldn't talk to the teacher before class.
2. We should / shouldn't visit Venice in the summer.
3. You should / shouldn't wear a tie with that shirt.
4. We should / shouldn't look for a hotel on the Internet.

 C **Pair work.** Tell your partner one thing people *should* do in each kind of weather and one thing they *shouldn't* do.

1. cold   2. cloudy   3. windy   4. sunny   5. warm

World Link

Lightning strikes the earth a hundred times every second, and kills more people (about 1,000 a year worldwide) than any other kind of storm, including hurricanes.

In cold weather, you should wear a sweater.

4 Speaking

You should take a sweater.

 A Read the conversation and listen. What does Juliet suggest taking to San Francisco? Why? (CD 1, Track 36)

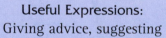

Juliet: Are you packing for your trip, Kyle?

Kyle: Yes . . . See? I have T-shirts, shorts, and my sandals.

Juliet: For San Francisco?

Kyle: Yeah. What's wrong? It's July.

Juliet: I know, but it's often foggy and cold there in the summer.

Kyle: Really?

Juliet: Yeah. You should take some sweaters and long pants, too.

Kyle: Oh, okay. There are some in my closet.

 B Pair work. Practice the conversation with your partner.

 C Pair work. Role play. Choose a situation below, and create a short role play. In your conversation, give advice and make suggestion. Use the Useful Expressions to help you.

Role-play situations

1. You and your partner are going to a party. It's snowing and the roads are icy. Your partner wants to drive.

2. Your partner wants to have a picnic. The weather forecast is predicting rain.

3. You and your partner are at the beach. It's a hot, sunny day. Your partner gets sunburned easily.

> **Useful Expressions:**
> Giving advice, suggesting
>
> It's chilly in the evening:
> You **should** take a sweater.
> **Why don't you** take a sweater?
>
> It's snowing:
> You **shouldn't** wear shorts.
> It's **not a good idea** to drive.

D Group work. Work in a group of three or four.

- Think of a problem you are having. Write it on a piece of paper.
- Read your problem to the group. People take turns giving advice. Which advice is the best? Why?

> Come on, Angie. The party starts in ten minutes, and it's snowing. We should take a cab . . .

> A cab? I don't want to . . .

5 Language Link

Connecting sentences with *but, or, so*

A Study the chart. Then complete the sentences below with *but, or,* or *so.*

It's cold **but** sunny in Vancouver today. It's cold in Boston, **but** it's warm in Miami.	• shows an opposite or contrast • joins words and sentences
Is it warm **or** chilly today? It's very hot! I can't eat **or** sleep. We can go to the beach, **or** we can visit the zoo.	• gives a choice • joins words and sentences
It's raining, **so** we're not having a picnic in the park.	• gives a result, joins sentences

1. William can't speak French, _____ Marion can.
2. Roberto is very healthy. He doesn't drink _____ smoke.
3. I feel tired, _____ I'm going home.
4. Does the movie start at 7:00 _____ 7:30?
5. Tokyo is an exciting city, _____ it's very expensive to live in.
6. The computer is broken, _____ I can't check my e-mail.
7. It's cold outside, _____ Mario is wearing shorts.
8. For dinner, you can have chicken, fish, _____ beef.

B Combine the two sentences using *but, or,* or *so.*

1. Damon likes to travel. His girlfriend doesn't like to travel.
   Damon likes to travel, but his girlfriend doesn't._____

2. We can go to Martin's party. We can see a movie.
   _____

3. John is sick. He's not coming to class today.
   _____

4. It's a beautiful day. We're having class outside.
   _____

5. I'm wearing my glasses. I can't see the whiteboard.
   _____

6. Alain wants to study at an American university. He's taking the TOEFL exam.
   _____

C **Pair work.** Complete the sentences about yourself. Then read each sentence
to a partner. Your partner asks you one question about each sentence.

1. I can _____, but I can't _____.
2. I like to _____ or _____ in the summer.
3. The weather here is often _____ in the winter, so _____.

A **Pair work.** Interview your partner. Compete the survey with his or her answers.

Vacation Survey

1. When do you usually take a vacation?

☐ in the spring ☐ in the autumn

☐ in the summer ☐ in the winter

2. What kind of weather do you like?

☐ hot ☐ warm ☐ cool

3. On a vacation, what do you like to do?

☐ relax ☐ exercise ☐ see things

4. What are your favorite activities?

☐ swimming ☐ hiking
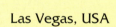

☐ skiing ☐ playing golf

☐ surfing ☐ cycling
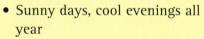

 B **Pair work.** Imagine that your partner is looking for a place to go on vacation. Read about the places below and choose one for your partner.

Cape Town, South Africa

Weather:
- In spring and summer (September–March), it's warm.
- The autumn and winter months are chilly, and it rains.

Activities: This coastal city has beautiful mountains and lively beaches. They're great for
- hiking   • surfing
- swimming   • relaxing
- waterskiing

Las Vegas, USA

Weather:
- Sunny days, cool evenings all year
- In summer, it's 100°F/38°C

Activities:
- casinos, great nightlife and restaurants
- swimming pools and golf courses.
- beautiful mountains for hiking, and for skiing and snowboarding in winter.

Montreal, Canada

Weather:
- It's hot and humid in summer.
- It's about 23°F/-5°C in winter.
- Spring and autumn are nice.

Activities:
- Skiing is popular in winter.
- In spring and summer, Mont Royal Park is great for hiking and cycling.
- relaxing cafés and hip nightclubs—often compared to Paris

 C **Pair work.** Tell your partner your suggestion. Explain your reasons. Does your partner like your suggestion?

You should go to Las Vegas or Cape Town. You like warm weather, but you usually have a vacation in December . . .

 D **Pair work.** Change partners, and do activities A to C again.

Vacation!

Lesson B | On vacation

When you travel

A Imagine that you are going on vacation to another country. Match an activity with a photo.

a. pack your suitcase	d. go sightseeing	g. show photos to friends
b. check into your hotel	e. get a passport	h. rent a car
c. buy a plane ticket	f. take photos	i. unpack

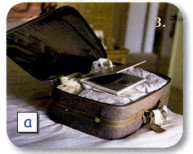

B **Pair work.** Which activities do you do before you travel? Which do you do on vacation? Which ones do you do after the trip? Tell your partner.

> *Before you travel to another country, you get a passport. On vacation, you go sightseeing . . .*

ask **&** ANSWER

How often do you go on vacation? Do you have a passport? Why or why not? On vacation, do you take a lot of photos?

A Listen to these three conversations. What is each person doing? Circle the correct answer. (CD 1, Track 37)

1. The woman is buying a plane ticket / getting a passport / checking in at the airport.
2. The man and woman are taking / showing a photo of the Statue of Liberty.
3. The man is renting a car / getting a passport / checking into a hotel.

 B Listen again. Complete the sentences with the correct city. (CD 1, Track 38)

1. The woman is traveling to _____.
2. The man and woman are in _____.
3. The man and woman are visiting _____.

World Link

The Statue of Liberty was presented to the U.S. in 1886 as a gift of international friendship from the people of France.

ask&
ANSWER

Look at your answers in B. Which place would you like to visit? Why?

3 Reading

Lost and found

When you travel, do you ever forget things in your hotel or at the airport? What do you forget?

 A Study the pictures of these items. Then read the news story on page 53 and underline the items in the story. How are these five things related to each other?

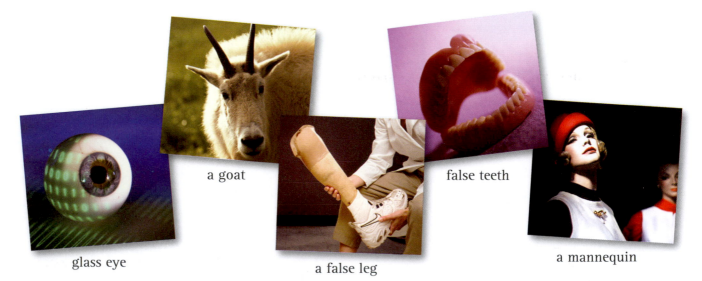

glass eye

a goat

a false leg

false teeth

a mannequin

Lost and Found

¹ In Tokyo, it's an envelope with $850,000 in cash. At Florida's Disney World, it's a glass eye. At a hotel in England, it's a goat and a false leg. How ⁵ are all of these things similar? They are unusual things that people leave in hotel rooms, in airports, and on city streets.

Trish Martino works in the Lost and Found Center at an airport in a US city. ¹⁰ "Sure, we find the usual stuff—cell phones, keys, sunglasses, and wallets," she says. "But people also forget some weird things at the airport, too." What does Ms. Martino find? A woman's false ¹⁵ teeth in the bathroom. A mannequin in an airport waiting area. "How do you forget those things?" Martino wonders.

Nobuo Hasuda works for the Lost and Found Center in downtown Tokyo. ²⁰ The Center has almost 800,000 items. Three hundred thousand of them are umbrellas! There are also many other things—jewelry and briefcases, snowshoes and musical instruments.

²⁵ Mr. Hasuda keeps the lost items for six months and two weeks. After this time, the finder can take the item. This is good luck for some people. Remember the envelope in Tokyo with $850,000? The ³⁰ owner did not claim it. Now the money belongs to the finder!

B **Read the story again. Then complete each sentence with the correct word or number.**

1. In Tokyo, someone lost $_____ in cash.
2. In England, someone forgot a _____ and a _____ in a hotel room.
3. People often lose these things in US airports: _____, _____, _____, and _____.
4. Tokyo's Lost and Found downtown center has _____ umbrellas.
5. In Tokyo, if the owner doesn't claim the lost item, the _____ can ask for it.

C **Find these words in the reading.**

1. This word in line 10 means objects or things: _____.
2. This word in line 13 means strange or unusual: _____.
3. This word in line 30 means to ask for a lost item: _____.

ask&ANSWER

Imagine that you find $850,000.
Complete the sentence with your ideas:
I am going to _____
_____.

review

4 Language Link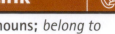

Whose; possessive pronouns; belong to

A Study the chart. Notice the words in bold.

Whose passport is this?	Possessive adjectives	Possessive pronouns	*belong to*
	It's **my** passport.	It's **mine.**	It **belongs to me.**
	your	**yours.**	**you.**
	her	**hers.**	**her.**
	his	**his.**	**him.**
	your	**ours.**	**us.**
	their	**theirs.**	**them.**

B **Group work.** Work in groups of three. Complete the conversation with the correct words. Use the chart above to help you. Then practice the conversation.

Jim: OK, Bobby. I have my luggage. Where's (1) _yours_?

Bobby: I don't know. Oh wait, here's (2) _mine_ suitcase.

Jim: Great. Let's go.

Bobby: Wait a minute. This suitcase isn't (3) _my_.

Jim: Are you sure?

Bobby: Yeah, it says *Simon Konig.*

Jim: Hey, I think that guy over there has (4) _suitcase_. Maybe this one is (5) _his_.

Bobby: Excuse me, sir. Does this suitcase belong to (6) _you_?

Simon: Yes, thanks. It's (7) _me_. And I think this one is (8) _mine_.

C Answer the questions using possessive pronouns and *belong to.*

1. Whose ticket is this? (Mary's) ___It's hers. It belongs to her.___
2. Whose keys are these? (my keys) _It's mine. It belong to me._
3. Whose suitcase is this? (my parents') _It's theirs. It belong to them._
4. Whose sunglasses are these? (John's) _his_
5. Whose car is this? (Peter's and mine) _____

D **Group work.** Read the directions to do this activity.

1. Student A closes his or her eyes.
2. Each of the other students chooses a personal item and puts it on Student A's desk.
3. Student A opens his or her eyes.
4. Student A guesses the owner of each item.
5. Repeat the activity with a different Student A.

Is this your watch?

No, it's not mine.

Whose is it?

I don't know. Maybe it's hers.

5 Writing

Newspaper ad

 A Read the ad below. Then write an ad about a lost item of yours.

 LOST!

Brown leather backpack. Two university textbooks are inside—one is a math textbook; the other is a history book. Lost at a bus stop near Georgetown University on Monday night. Please contact the owner at 555-2121. $50 reward!

 B **Class activity.** Put your ad on the classroom wall. Read the other ads. Are any of the ads similar? What kinds of things do most people lose?

6 Communication

Are we compatible?

A Complete the survey below with your answers.

On vacation . . .	My answer	My partner's answer
1. How do you like to travel—by bus, plane, train, or car?		
2. How many suitcases do you usually take?		
3. What is something you always take? What is something you never take?		
4. Do you spend a lot of money?		
5. Do you like to travel by yourself or go with a group?		
6. Do you like to take a lot of pictures?		
7. Do you like to go sightseeing or relax?		

B **Pair work.** Get together with a partner. Take turns asking and answering the questions. Explain your answers.

C Are you and your partner similar or different? Do you think you could travel together? Why or why not? Tell the class.

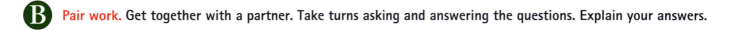
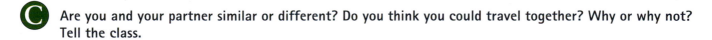

Check out the World Link video.   **Practice your English online at http://elt.thomson.com/worldlink**

6 All About You

Lesson A | My favorite pastimes

1 Vocabulary Link

Teams and clubs

A Match a word in the box with an activity on the web page.

a. ~~baseball~~
b. soccer
c. basketball
d. chess
e. rowing
f. volleyball
g. swimming
h. tennis
i. bowling

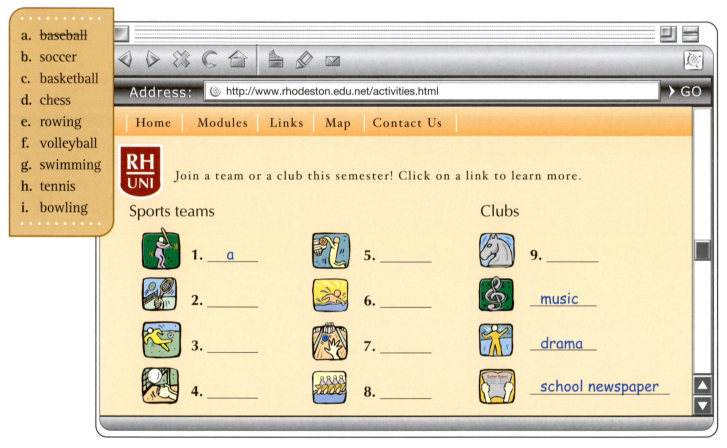

Address: http://www.rhodeston.edu.net/activities.html ⟩ GO

Home | Modules | Links | Map | Contact Us

RH UNI Join a team or a club this semester! Click on a link to learn more.

Sports teams

1. _a_
2. _____
3. _____
4. _____

5. _____
6. _____
7. _____
8. _____

Clubs

9. _____
music
drama
school newspaper

B **Pair work.** With a partner, match each noun from the box in **A** with a verb below.

baseball — play   swimming — go

C **Pair work.** What other activities match with *go* and *play*? Add them to the list.

ask & ANSWER
Look at the web page. Which clubs or teams are interesting to you? Why?

2 Listening

Whose trophies are these?

  A Listen. Circle the correct answer to complete the sentence. (CD 1, Track 39)

Mike / Mike's family has a lot of trophies.

B Listen again. Which sports do they play? Check (✓) the correct box or boxes. (CD 1, Track 40)

	surfing	golf	swimming	basketball	skiing	tennis
brother	☐	☐	☐	☐	☐	☐
sister	☐	☐	☐	☐	☐	☐
dad	☐	☐	☐	☐	☐	☐
mom	☐	☐	☐	☐	☐	☐
Mike	☐	☐	☐	☐	☐	☐

ask & ANSWER

Do you, or does someone you know, play a sport?
Do you have any awards or trophies? Explain.

 **World Link**

Early versions of the modern game of chess were played in China and India over 2,000 years ago.

  ## 3 Pronunciation

Reduced *to*

 A The pronunciation of *to* is usually reduced. Listen to these sentences. Notice the weak, short pronunciation of *to*. (CD 1, Track 41)

1. I like to play golf.
2. She likes to go jogging.
3. I love to sleep late.
4. He hates to study.
5. We plan to fly to Paris.
6. Do you like to play chess?
7. I want to be early.
8. I hate to be late.

B **Pair work.** Practice saying the sentences in **A** with your partner. Pay attention to the pronunciation of *to.*

A Listen to the conversation. Underline Gina's invitation. Circle the words Connie uses to accept Gina's invitation. (CD 1, Track 42)

Connie:	So, Gina, are you planning to join a team or club this semester?
Gina:	Yeah. I want to work for the school newspaper and maybe join the tennis team.
Connie:	The tennis team?
Gina:	Uh-huh. Do you like tennis?
Connie:	Yes, I love it.
Gina:	Really? Me too. Do you want to play tennis this afternoon?
Connie:	Sure, I'd love to! There are tennis courts near the student union. Let's play there.

B **Pair work.** Practice the conversation with your partner.

C Think of a sport or activity you like to do. Complete the information below.

1. Sport or activity I like to do: _____
2. Place to do the sport or activity: _____
3. Day/time I want to do the activity: _____

> **Places to do sports/activities**
>
> tennis court
> basketball court
> bowling alley
> swimming pool
> soccer field

D **Pair work.** Invite four people in your class to do your activity in C. They can accept or decline the invitation. Use the Useful Expressions to help you.

> *Do you want to go bowling after class? There's a bowling alley at the mall.*

> *Sorry, I can't. I'm busy.*

> *Sure, I'd love to go!*

Useful Expressions:
Inviting; accepting and declining invitations
Do you want to play tennis this afternoon?
Sure, I'd love to!
Sorry, I can't. I'm busy.
Thanks, but . . . (I can't play tennis).

Verb + noun; verb + infinitive

 A Study the chart. Notice the verbs and the highlighted words.

I love baseball. It's my favorite sport. I want a new car. I don't like spicy food.	A noun or noun phrase can follow many verbs.
I love to play tennis. I want to buy a new car. Do you plan to visit Australia?	The infinitive can follow some verbs. Some of these are *like, love, hate, want, plan,* and *expect.*

B Read the sentences. Underline the main verb. Is the main verb followed by a noun or noun phrase or by an infinitive? Write *N* (for noun or noun phrase) or *I* (for infinitive).

1. I <u>like</u> to swim.   I
2. Connor likes this video game.   _____
3. Diane wants a new swimsuit.   _____
4. Does he want to play tennis?   _____
5. We love to watch old movies.   _____

6. I hate loud music.   _____
7. No, I don't want more coffee.   _____
8. He expects to do well on the test.   _____
9. Nadia doesn't like baseball.   _____
10. I plan to buy the blue hat.   _____

C This is Jenna. For each picture, make up two sentences about her. Use the verbs *like, want,* and *love.* Write your sentences on a separate piece of paper.

 D **Pair work.** Read your ideas to your partner. Are they the same?

Jenna likes to ski.

 ask& **ANSWER**

What's your favorite sport or game? Which sports or games don't you like?
What kind of music do you love? What music don't you like?
What movie do you want to see? What movie don't you want to see?

A Read the questions below. Write your answers under *My answer* in the chart.

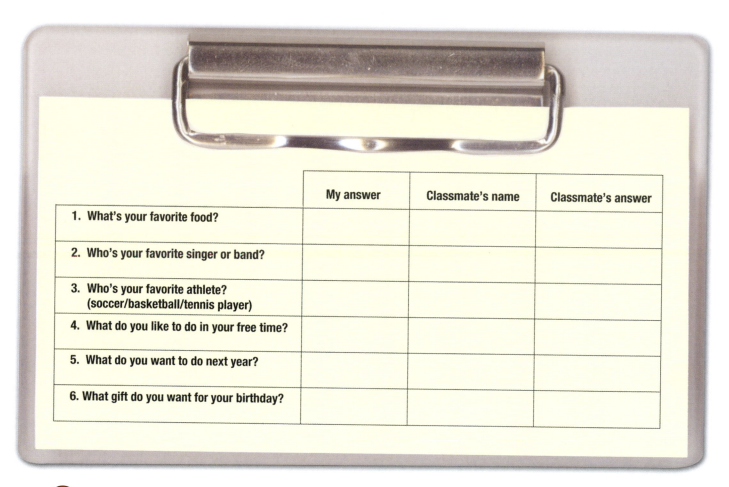

	My answer	Classmate's name	Classmate's answer
1. What's your favorite food?			
2. Who's your favorite singer or band?			
3. Who's your favorite athlete? (soccer/basketball/tennis player)			
4. What do you like to do in your free time?			
5. What do you want to do next year?			
6. What gift do you want for your birthday?			

B **Class activity.** For each question, interview a *different* classmate. Write each person's name and answer in the chart.

C **Group work.** Join a group of three people. For each question, read a classmate's answer. Do *not* say the person's name. Your group guesses which classmate gave that answer.

OK, first question. What's your person's favorite food?

This person loves spicy food—especially hot curry!

I know! That's Mateo.

Yes, that's right!

All About You

1 Vocabulary Link

What's she like?

 A Look at the picture of Kira's apartment. Then read the sentences below. Pay attention to the highlighted adjectives.

1. Kira is independent. She has her own apartment and pays her own bills.
2. She is a serious, hardworking student. She gets all As.
3. She's creative. She loves to paint, and has many new ideas.
4. Kira is not very organized. Her desk is very messy.
5. Kira likes to play sports. She's very competitive. She likes to win.
6. Kira has a lot of credit card bills. She's not careful with her money. She goes shopping and buys things without thinking. She's impulsive.

B Match the sentences in A with a place in the apartment. Write the number (1–6) in the circle.

C Which adjectives in A describe you? Your parents? Your best friend? Explain with an example.

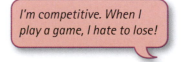
I'm competitive. When I play a game, I hate to lose!

2 Listening

A conversation with Dad

 A Listen. What are Ashley and her dad talking about? Check the correct answer. (CD 1, Track 43)

☐ Ashley's grades   ☐ Ashley's major at school   ☐ Ashley's part-time job

 B Listen again. Complete the sentences. (CD 1, Track 44)

1. Ashley wants to study art / business.
2. Her dad wants her to study art / business.
3. Ashley says there is very little / a lot she can do with an art degree.
4. Ashley thinks the business world is perfect / too competitive for her.

ANSWER
Who do you agree with—Ashley or her dad? Explain.

World Link

The world's oldest university Al-Azhar University is in Cairo, Egypt. The first lecture was given there in 975 A.D.

3 Reading

What's your personality type?

The reading on page 63 talks about four personality types: *The Dreamer, The Partner, The Thinker,* and *The Artist.* Look only at these four names. Which one describes you?

 A Read the magazine article on page 63. Which personality type are you?

 B Read the article again. Circle *D* for Dreamer, *P* for Partner, *T* for Thinker, or *A* for Artist for each sentence. Sometimes more than one answer is possible.

1. This person wants to be in a group.   D P T A
2. These people are often hardworking and organized.   D P T A
3. These people like to be free.   D P T A
4. These people are competitive.   D P T A
5. These people often work as teachers.   D P T A
6. These people often work as politicians.   D P T A
7. Lance Armstrong is an example of this personality type. D P T A
8. Harry Potter is an example of this personality type.   D P T A

ANSWER
Look again at the reading. For each personality type, think of one more famous person to add to the list. Explain your choice.

What is your personality type?

What is your personality type? Are you similar to Martin Luther King Jr. or Russell Crowe? Queen Elizabeth or Albert Einstein? Read about these types and find out!

The Dreamer

A Dreamer thinks there is a "right" way to do things. This person wants to live in the "perfect world." A Dreamer is often hardworking and organized. Many are good listeners and like to help others. Many Dreamers work as teachers, lawyers, and in leadership roles.

Famous Dreamers: Mohandas Gandhi, Martin Luther King Jr., Aung San Suu Kyi

The Partner

A Partner wants to be in a group. For this person, rules and group harmony are important. These rules keep peace in the group. Partners are often serious, careful people. Many do well as teachers, managers, police officers, and politicians.

Famous Partners: Queen Elizabeth II, Mother Teresa

The Thinker

For Thinkers, understanding things is very important. They like to solve problems and make new things. Thinkers can also be competitive. They like to win. They are independent and often have very strong opinions. Many Thinkers work as scientists, inventors, politicians, and engineers.

Famous Thinkers: Bill Gates, Socrates, Albert Einstein

The Artist

Artists want to be free. They don't want to follow the rules all the time. Artists like action and are often impulsive. They also like trying new things. Like Thinkers, many Artists have strong opinions. Many Artists are creative and do well as musicians, actors, fashion designers, and athletes.

Famous Artists: Russell Crowe, Madonna, Lance Armstrong

4 Language Link

How often . . . ?; frequency expressions

A **Pair work.** Study the chart. Then look at Ricardo's calendar. Take turns asking and answering questions about him with your partner.

> How often do you check your e-mail?
>
> Every day / Monday / week / month.   All the time. (very often)
> Once a week.   Once in a while. (sometimes)
> Twice a month.
> Three times a year.

How often does Ricardo . . .

1. have class? _____   3. work at the café? _____

2. meet with his study group? _____   4. work from 3:00–6:00? _____

MONTH	MON	TUE	WED	THU	FRI	SAT	SUN
	Class 9:00–noon	Work 10:00–2:00	Class 9:00–noon	Work 10:00–2:00	Class 9:00–noon	Work 1:00–4:00	Work 3:00–6:00
	Work 1:00–4:00	Study Group 4:00–6:00	Work 1:00–4:00	Study Group 4:00–6:00	Work 1:00–4:00		

B **Pair work.** Take turns asking and answering questions about these activities with your partner. Explain your answers.

> How often do you have class?

have class   go on a date   exercise
buy new clothes   check your e-mail   get a haircut

> Three times a week.

5 Writing

What are you like?

A Read Luisa's description. Then write about yourself. Choose two adjectives that describe your personality.

B **Pair work.** Exchange your paper with a partner's. Read your partner's description. Are you similar or different?

> Hi there! My name is Luisa.
> I am independent. I like to do things for myself.
> I like to make my own choices. I don't need other people's advice all the time. I am also open-minded.
> I like to learn and try new things. I like to hear othe[r] people's opinions and ideas.
> What about you? What are you like?

A **Pair work.** Use the chart to interview a partner. Circle his or her answers.

Personality Quiz

Questions	Answers	
How often do you clean your room?	a. once a week	b. once in a while. I hate to clean.
How often do friends ask for your advice?	a. all the time	b. almost never
What is more important?	a. being kind	b. being honest
What is more important?	a. agreeing with the group	b. saying my opinion
Are you careful with money?	a. Yes, almost always.	b. No, not really.
Which is important to you?	a. success	b. happiness
You're playing a game. Which sentence describes you?	a. I hate to lose.	b. I want to win, but if I lose, it's OK.
You cell phone isn't working. What do you do?	a. try to fix it myself	b. ask for help
What is more important?	a. facts	b. feelings
What do you want in your life?	a. many different experiences	b. the same job
What is more important?	a. being free	b. being careful
You get a free ticket to Paris. The plane leaves tomorrow. Do you go?	a. Yes!	b. No way!

B **Pair work.** Total your partner's points for each color (a = 2 points, b = 1 point). Read about the color(s) with the *most* points on page 154, and tell your partner about his or her personality type(s).

C **Pair work.** Do you agree with your description? Explain your opinion to your partner.

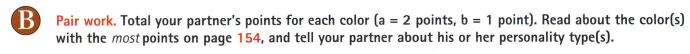
Check out the World Link video. **Practice your English online at http://elt.thomson.com/worldlink**

1 Storyboard

 A **Pair work.** Rolf and Brigit are visiting San Francisco. Look at the pictures and work with a partner to complete the conversations. More than one answer is possible for each blank.

B **Group work.** Practice the conversations. Then change roles and practice again.

Pair work. Study the picture below for 15 seconds. Then, close your book. What are the people doing? Tell your partner.

Some people are playing volleyball.

 Pair Work. Talk about the picture.

- Where are these people?
- What season is it? How's the weather?
- Invite your partner to do one of the activities in the picture.
- Do you know any vacation resorts like this one? Where are they? What are they like?

 Pair work. Choose one pair of people in the picture. With a partner, role-play a conversation between the two people.

A **Pair work.** Read the information. Then answer the questions below with a partner.

Miss Smith and Miss Jones are neighbors. Every afternoon, they have tea together.

At 4:00, Miss Jones goes to Miss Smith's apartment and knocks. This afternoon, Miss Smith doesn't answer the door. After many knocks, Miss Jones calls Mr. Busby, the apartment manager. He has a key to Miss Smith's apartment. He opens the door. Miss Smith is lying on the floor. She is dead.

The police come and search the apartment. They find an apartment key under the sofa. The key belongs to the killer. The number on the key is 300. Now the question is: who is the killer?

- Who are Miss Smith and Miss Jones?
- Who is Mr. Busby?
- What do Miss Jones and Mr. Busby see?
- What do the police find? Why is it important?

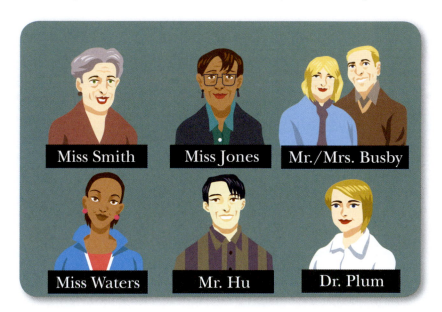

B **Pair work.** Work with your partner to find the killer. Try to be the first in the class.

Partner A: Read the sentences to your partner.

Miss Smith lives in apartment 305.

Mr. and Mrs. Busby live across from Miss Smith.

Ms. Waters lives between Miss Jones and Mr. and Mrs. Busby.

Mr. Hu lives across from Ms. Waters.

The apartment next to Miss Smith's is 303.

Mr. Hu lives next to Dr. Plum.

Dr. Plum lives across from apartment 300.

Let's see. Miss Smith lives in Apartment 305.

Miss Smith . . . 305 . . . OK, got it!

Partner B: Write the names and room numbers below.

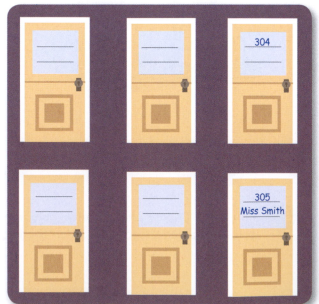

4 Listening: Who should get the job?

 A Sam and Lisa want to hire a swimming teacher.
Listen. Then complete the sentence. (CD 1, Track 45)

Sam and Lisa need a swimming instructor for _____.

    a. adults

    b. teens

    c. young children

Ally

Carl

 B **Listen again. Do these words describe Ally or Carl?**
Check (✓) the correct boxes. (CD 1, Track 46)

	is hardworking	is friendly	is on a swimming team	coaches a swim team	has experience	loves kids
Ally						
Carl						

 C **Pair work. Compare your answers in A and B with a partner.**
In your opinion, who should get the job? Why?

5 Speak for a minute!

 A **Read the questions and think about your answers.**

1. What's your favorite season? Why? What's the weather like?
2. Describe your neighborhood.
3. How often do you exercise, go to a gym, or play a sport?
4. How many friends do you have? What are they like?
5. How much TV do you watch?
6. What is something you love to do? How often do you do it?
7. How often do you eat in a restaurant? How much do you spend?
8. Use three words to describe yourself. Explain your three choices.
9. Name two places you would like to go on a vacation. Explain your choices.

 B **Group work. Get into a group of three people.**

1. Take turns. Choose a question, 1 to 9.
2. Answer the question by talking for one minute without stopping, and you get one point.
3. Continue until there are no more questions.
4. The winner is the person with the most points.

Change

Lesson A | I need a change.

1 Vocabulary Link

I need a change.

A These people want to change. Complete each sentence with a verb from the box. Some verbs can be used more than once.

a. get
b. quit
c. make
d. join
e. lose

I want to change my style.

You should
1. __get__ a haircut.

I want to get in shape.

You should
2. _____ a gym.
3. _____ weight.
4. _____ smoking.

I can't pay my bills!

You should
5. _____ more money.
6. _____ a better job.

I want to be more outgoing.

You should
7. _____ a club.

B **Pair work.** Tell your partner about changes you want to make in your life.

I want to get a haircut and quit smoking.

2 Listening

New Year's resolutions

On December 31, some people make New Year's resolutions. A New Year's resolution is a promise you make to do something different and positive.

  A Listen to the conversation. What are Mick's and Paula's New Year's resolutions? Circle the correct answers. (CD 2, Track 1)

1. Mick wants to make more money / get a new job.
2. Paula wants to study modern art / dance.

  B Listen again. Circle *True* or *False*. (CD 2, Track 2)

1. Mick wants a new job.	True	False
2. Mick doesn't make very much money.	True	False
3. In his job now, Mick works long hours.	True	False
4. Paula doesn't have a hobby.	True	False
5. Paula is taking a dance class now.	True	False

C Change the **false** sentences in **B** to make them true.

3 Pronunciation

Reduced *want to*

ask& ANSWER
Do you usually make New Year's resolutions? What kinds of resolutions do you make?

 A Listen to the sentences. Notice the pronunciation of *want to*. (CD 2, Track 3)

I want to get a haircut.
Julie and Ed want to rent a bigger apartment.

 B Listen to the conversation. Pay attention to the pronunciation of *want to*. (CD 2, Track 4)

A: What do you want to do tonight?
B: I don't want to stay home. Let's see a movie.
A: OK. What do you want to see?
B: There's a good movie at the Strand Theater. Do Eric and Sue want to come with us?
A: They're not home. They're taking a language class. They want to learn to speak Italian.

 **World** Link

Many cultures share the custom of making New Year's resolutions, but not all celebrate New Year's Day on January 1. Chinese people, for example, celebrate it in late January or early February.

C Pair work. Practice the conversation with a partner. Pay attention to your pronunciation of *want to*.

A Listen to the conversation. What does Zack want from Juan? How does he ask for it? (CD 2, Track 5)

Zack:	See you later, Juan. I'm going out for a while.
Juan:	OK, see you.
Zack:	Oh no!
Juan:	What?
Zack:	I forgot to go to the ATM.
Juan:	Do you need money?
Zack:	Yeah, I'd like to get a haircut this afternoon. Can I borrow $20?
Juan:	Sure, here you go.
Zack:	Thanks a lot.

B **Pair work.** Practice the conversation with a partner.

C **Pair work.** Choose an item from the box. Ask to borrow it from your partner and give a reason. Use the Useful Expressions to help you create a conversation.

> your partner's cell phone   your partner's car
> your partner's shoes   your idea: _____
> some money

Wendy, could I borrow your cell phone for a minute?

My cell phone? Why?

Useful Expressions: Making and responding to requests
Can I borrow your cell phone? I need to call my parents.
Could I borrow . . . ?
Can you lend me . . . ?
Could you lend me . . . ?

Positive responses	Negative response
Sure. No problem. Certainly.	I'm sorry, but . . . (+ reason).

 D **Pair work.** Change roles and create conversations for all the items in C.

5 Language Link

Like to **vs.** *would like to*

I'd = I would

 Pair work. Read the sentences. Notice the underlined words.
Then answer the questions below with a partner.

a. I <u>like to</u> visit Australia.
My favorite place is Bondi Beach.

b. I<u>'d like to</u> visit Australia next summer.

Which sentence . . .

1. means *I enjoy visiting Australia?*   a   b
2. means *I want to visit Australia?*   a   b

3. talks about a future desire?   a   b

B Read the questions. Then circle the correct words to complete each answer.

1. What do you usually do on the weekend?
   I like to / I'd like to relax.

2. Why is Pedro studying Japanese?
   He likes to / He'd like to learn languages.

3. Why are you studying for the TOEFL exam?
   I like to / I'd like to study in the United States.

4. What's your New Year's resolution?
   I like to / I'd like to get in shape.

5. How was your vacation to Brazil?
   We loved it! We like to / We'd like to visit again.

6. Do your parents both work?
   Yes, but they like to / they'd like to retire soon.

C Write sentences about yourself. Start each with *I like to* or *I'd like to.*

1. Name something you like to do in your free time.
   _____

2. Name something you'd like to do in your life.
   _____

3. Name a TV show you like to watch.
   _____

4. Name a movie you'd like to see.
   _____

5. Name one place tourists like to visit in your city.
   _____

6. Name one thing you'd like to change about your city.
   _____

 Pair work. Take turns talking about your answers in **C** with a partner.

A Pair work. Look at the lists of bad habits and bad qualities below. Can you add other ideas to the lists? Tell your partner.

BAD HABITS	BAD QUALITIES

I bite my nails.
    spend too much money.
    eat a lot of junk food.
    talk on the phone too much.
    watch too much TV.
	I'm messy.
	     lazy.
	     late all the time.

B Pair work. Look at the pictures with a partner. What bad habits and bad qualities do these people have?

 C Pair work. Role play.
Student A: Imagine that you are the person in picture 1 above. Tell your partner about your bad habits and bad qualities. Ask your partner for advice on how to change.
Student B: Listen to your partner. Suggest ways that he or she can change.

> *I have a lot of bills! I'd like to save money, but I can't! What can I do?*

> *Well, don't use your credit cards. It's too easy to spend money.*

 D Pair work. Switch roles and do another role play.
Student B is the person in picture 2 above.

Change

1 Vocabulary Link

Graduation plans

A Read about these college seniors' dreams for the future. Pay attention to the words in blue.

Dreams of Life After College

Pilar

Darryl

Yeny

Justin

After graduation, I want to go to medical school. I want to **become** a doctor.

I want to **move** to New York City, and become a **successful** chef. I want to have my **own** restaurant someday.

After graduation, my **goal** is to get a good job. I'd also like to **get married**—but not until I'm 30!

What are my goals after graduation? I don't know! First, I want to **take a break** and travel.

B Use the blue words and phrases from A in the sentences below. Then check answers with a partner.

1. A: What's your _____*goal*_____ this year? B: I want to lose five kilos.
2. I'm really tired. Let's _____. We can finish the homework later.
3. Mr. Suzuki is a very _____ businessman. He has restaurants all over Japan.
4. Mei's dorm room is very small. She wants to _____ to a larger room.
5. Javier wants to _____ a very rich man.
6. We're renting an apartment, but we'd like to have our _____ house in the future.
7. Jane loves her boyfriend, but she doesn't want to _____ now. She wants to focus on her career.

Look again at the four seniors' plans. Would you like to do any of these things? Why or why not?

2 Listening

Follow your dreams

  A Listen to the first part of this radio interview and circle the correct answers. (CD 2, Track 6)

1. Yeliz is a successful actress / singer / guitarist.
2. Yeliz is American / Turkish / Scottish.
3. Yeliz is 17 / 21 / 25 years old.
4. In her job, Yeliz doesn't travel very much / travels a lot.

 B Listen again. Complete the sentences. Check (✓) the correct boxes. (CD 2, Track 7)

1. Yeliz thinks her life is ☐ a little boring. ☐ pretty exciting.

2. After the tour, Yeliz plans to ☐ take a break. ☐ make a new CD.

3. Yeliz's advice to young artists is: ☐ Follow your dreams. ☐ Make new goals.

4. Yeliz says, "Work hard, and you can be ☐ happy." ☐ successful."

ask **&**
ANSWER
What do you think of Yeliz's advice to young artists?
Do you agree with her? Why or why not?

3 Reading

A lifetime dream

World Link

Teenage boys and girls have different dream jobs, according to a U.S. survey. 47% of boys aged 15-19 rank being a "tester for new video games" as their dream summer job, while 36% of teen girls would most like to be a "personal shopper at a major clothing store."

 What is your "dream job"?

A Read the sentences below. Then quickly look at the magazine article on page 77 to find the answers.

1. Yi Wang wants to be a teacher / make films.
2. Hicham Nassir wants to play soccer / be a lawyer.

B Now read the magazine article carefully.

C Complete each sentence with the correct word or words from the reading.

1. Yi Wang is a _____ teacher at a university in Beijing.
2. Wang's biggest problem now is _____.
3. Someday, Wang and her partners want to show their film in _____ and _____.
4. Hicham Nassir's parents want him to study _____ or _____.
5. Hicham hopes his parents will _____.

Address: http://www.newszine.net ›GO

HOME   LATEST NEWS   INTERVIEWS   LINKS   CONTACT US

NEWS FROM A SMALL PLANET

A lifetime dream

This week, Jennifer Reece profiles the dreams of a Chinese professor and a Moroccan high school student.

"At the moment, I'm teaching chemistry at a university in Beijing. It's a good job, but my dream is to make films," says 29-year-old Yi Wang. "In China, young artists move to Beijing from all over the country. Many of them are painters, writers, and actors. I'd like to make a film about their lives and their work."

Wang is writing the film now with help from her friends. But it isn't easy. "At the moment, the biggest problem is money," explains Wang. "We don't have much."

But this isn't going to stop Wang and her partners. "First, we're going to make this movie. Then, we'd like to show it in China, and maybe someday, at film festivals around the world."

Click here to read more . . .

16-year-old Hicham Nassir is getting ready for a soccer match with his teammates. Hicham, the team's star player, is a native of Morocco. He now lives in London with his family.

"My parents want me to go to college, and major in business or law," he explains. "They want me to become a lawyer or a successful businessman. I understand them, but I want to be a pro soccer player. And my coach thinks I can do it."

And what about his parents? "I hope they change their minds," says Hicham. "I want to play soccer professionally. It's my dream."

Click here to read more . . .

ask**&**
ANSWER

Talk about a lifetime dream of yours. What's something you would like to do? Hicham Nassir's parents want him to go to college. Do your parents agree with your choices in life? Explain with an example.

4 Language Link

The future with *be going to*

> Going to is often said as *gonna*.
> Don't use *gonna* in writing.

A Study the sentences in the chart. Notice the verb form.

subject + *be*		*going to*	verb		
I'm					tomorrow.
You're					this summer.
He's/She's	not	going to	visit	Mexico	next month/year/summer.
We're					in two years.
They're					after graduation.

B Complete each sentence with *be going to* and the verb in parentheses.

1. I (visit) ___'m going to visit___ Italy this summer. I already have my plane ticket!
2. Barry (not go) _____ to class today. He's sick.
3. I think Tim (be) _____ at the party.
4. My parents (drive) _____ to Miami from New York.
5. We (not go) _____ to the movies tonight. We need to study.
6. I'm sure you (do) _____ well on the test. Don't worry!

C **Pair work.** Study the chart. Then, use *be going to* to complete the questions and answers in the conversation. Practice the conversation with a partner.

Yes/No question	**Are you going to visit** Mexico this summer?
	Yes, I am.
	Yes, maybe.
	No, I'm not.
Wh-question	**What are you going to do** this summer?
	I'm going to visit Mexico.

Elliot: Jo! Guess what? I won the newspaper trip!

Jo: The trip around the world? That's great news, Elliot!

Elliot: I know.

Jo: So, (1. when / you / go) ___when are you going to go___?

Elliot: Next month.

Jo: (2. you / take) _____ anyone?

Elliot: Yes, I am. (3. My roommate / come) _____ with me.

Jo: (4. Where / you / start) _____ the trip?

Elliot: First, (5. we / fly) _____ to London and spend a week there.

Jo: And after that? (6. Where / you / go) _____?

Elliot: Then (7. we / go) _____ to Paris, Rome, Madrid, Cape Town, Bangkok, Tokyo, and about ten other places.

Jo: Wow, how exciting. Send postcards!

5 Writing

My dream

A Read the paragraphs below. Then write about your dream. Don't write your name on your paper.

My dream is to run in the New York City Marathon. It's in November every year. I'm not going to run this year, but I'd like to enter next year.

I think the New York City Marathon is going to be difficult. It's twenty-six miles! To prepare, I'm going to train for six months. I know I'm not going to win the race. I just want to finish it!

B Class activity. Give your paper to your teacher. Your teacher gives you another student's paper. Read the paper you get. Guess the writer.

6 Communication

Plans for the future

A What are your plans for the near and distant future? Answer the questions in the chart. Then add one more.

Are you going to . . .	Yes, I am.	Maybe.	Probably not.	No, I'm not.
do something fun this weekend?				
continue to study English?				
take the TOEFL exam?				
move to another city?				
get married?				
have your own home?				
visit another country?				
learn another language?				
start your own business?				
_____?				

B Pair work. Take turns asking and answering the Yes/No questions in A with a partner. After each answer, ask your partner a Wh-question.

Are you going to do something fun this weekend?

Yes, I am.

What are you going to do?

 Check out the World Link video.   **Practice your English online at http://elt.thomson.com/worldlink**

Heroes

Lesson A | Heroes from the past

1 Vocabulary Link

People I admire

 A Pair work. Read about these people's heroes. Pay attention to the words in blue. Do you think the people in the photos are heroes? Tell your partner.

I admire firefighters. Their job is dangerous but they're not afraid. They're very brave.
– Maya, 32

Superman is my hero. He's brave and strong. He fights evil people— bad guys like Lex Luther.
– Devin, 12

Anne Frank was a hero. Her diary about hiding from the Nazis is famous. She was an intelligent and a brave young woman.
– Gabby, 21

In my opinion, Gandhi was a hero. He was a great leader. He helped to free his people.
– Simon, 47

B Circle the correct word or phrase to complete each sentence.

1. I really *admire* Phil. He's a very hardworking / lazy person.
2. A waiter's / police officer's job is usually *dangerous*.
3. Mia is a very *brave* person. She is afraid of a lot of things / isn't afraid of anything.
4. You have to be *strong* to lift this box. It weighs 25 / 2 kilos.
5. Many people think that Adolph Hitler / Princess Diana was an *evil* person.
6. Jo is an *intelligent* child. She's two years old, and she can write simple sentences / say "mama."
7. On an airplane, the flight attendant / pilot is the *leader*.

 C Pair work. For each item below, share your ideas with a partner. Explain your choices.

Name another . . .
1. brave person
2. dangerous job
3. strong person
4. great leader
5. intelligent person

 Who do you think is a brave person?

My dad. He isn't afraid of anything . . .

A Greg and Claudia are talking about a holiday in the United States. Listen. Which leader are they talking about? Check (✓) the photo. (CD 2, Track 8)

  B Listen again. Complete the sentences. Circle the correct answer. (CD 2, Track 9)

1. This leader's birthday is in January / June.
2. He was an important leader in the 1960s / 1970s.
3. His *I have a dream* song / speech is famous.
4. On the holiday, most people remember his teachings / go to large parades.

ask & ANSWER
Name a holiday that celebrates a national leader or hero. When is the holiday? What do people do on this day?

  A Listen to these sentences. Notice the pronunciation of *was, wasn't, were,* and *weren't.* (CD 2, Track 10)

1. Marie Curie **was** a famous scientist.   She **wasn't** born in France.
2. Where **were** you last night?   Why **weren't** you at home?

  B Listen. Circle the word you hear. (CD 2, Track 11)

1. That was / wasn't an interesting movie.
2. They were / weren't born in Japan.
3. In high school, my favorite subject was / wasn't history.
4. Kylie's parents were / weren't teachers at the International School.
5. Why were / weren't Inez and Margarita in class today?
6. I was / wasn't at home last night to get your call.

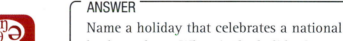

World Link

At age 35, civil rights leader Martin Luther King Jr. was the youngest man to receive a Nobel Peace Prize. Other famous winners include Nelson Mandela and Kim Dae-Jung.

 C Pair work. Practice saying the sentences in B with a partner.

4 Speaking

That was a good movie.

 A Listen to the conversation. What is Maggie writing about? Who is Yu Shu Lien? (CD 2, Track 12)

Kurt:	Hey Maggie, do you want to have lunch?
Maggie:	Thanks, but I can't now. I'm writing a paper about heroes in the movies.
Kurt:	That's interesting. Who are you writing about?
Maggie:	Yu Shu Lien. She was Michelle Yeoh's character in the film *Crouching Tiger, Hidden Dragon*.
Kurt:	Oh yeah. That was a good movie.
Maggie:	Yeah, I agree.
Kurt:	So, why is she your choice?
Maggie:	Well, she was a brave, strong woman.
Kurt:	Hey, let's rent that movie tonight.
Maggie:	Great idea! I'd like to see it again.

 B Pair work. Practice the conversation with a partner.

 C Complete the chart with information about two movie heroes you know.

	Hero	Movie	Is it a good movie?
1.			☐ Yes ☐ No
2.			☐ Yes ☐ No

D Pair work. Discuss your ideas in **C** with a partner. Use the Useful Expressions to help you.

> **Useful Expressions:**
> **Agreeing and disagreeing**
>
> I think *The Matrix* is a good movie.
>> Yeah, I agree.
>> Yeah, you're right.
>> I think so, too.
>> Sorry, but I disagree. In my opinion . . .
>> I don't really agree. I think . . .

Neo, The Matrix

The hero of The Matrix *was Neo. I think* The Matrix *is a great movie!*

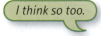 *I think so too.*

A Read the sentences in the chart. Pay attention to the verb forms.

subject	be		
I He/She	was wasn't	married	last year/summer. in 1999.
You We They	were weren't	in Toronto	two years ago.

 B **Pair work.** Complete the conversation with a partner. Use the correct form of the verb *be* in the past tense.

Kelly: Hello?

Tim: Hi. It's Tim. I called you four times yesterday, but you (not) **(1)** _____ home.

Kelly: I **(2)** _____ at the library. I'm writing a paper about Pierre and Marie Curie.

Tim: They **(3)** _____ scientists from France, right?

Kelly: Right. Well, actually Pierre **(4)** _____ French, but his wife (not) **(5)** _____ born in France. She **(6)** _____ from Poland.

Tim: Oh?

Kelly: Yeah. She **(7)** _____ also the first person to win a Nobel Prize twice.

C Complete the five questions about astronaut Yuri Gagarin.

1. <u>Where was he</u> _____ from?
2. _____ married or single?
3. _____ born?
4. _____ occupation?
5. _____ he famous?

I got a Job

Yes/No questions
Were you born in Mexico?
Yes, I was.
No, I wasn't. I was born in Chile.

Wh- questions
Where were you born?
(I was born) In Mexico.
Why was Marie Curie famous?
She was the first person to win a Nobel Prize twice.

D **Pair work.** Read about Yuri Gagarin. Then ask and answer the questions from **C** with a partner.

YURI GAGARIN
BIRTHPLACE: RUSSIA
BIRTH DATE: SEPTEMBER 3, 1934
OCCUPATION: ASTRONAUT
WHY FAMOUS: HE WAS THE FIRST
PERSON IN SPACE
(APRIL 1961)

MARRIED
OR SINGLE: MARRIED

6 Communication

Who was she?

 A You are going to play a game. Read the answers then complete the questions.

1. Was _the person male or female_____? This person was female.
2. Where _____? She was from Egypt.
3. When _____? She was born over 2,000 years ago.
4. Was _____? Yes, she was a famous leader.
5. What _____? Her name was . . .

 B Pair work. Ask and answer the questions in A. Who was this famous person? Tell your partner. Check your answer on page 154.

 C Group work. Get into a group of three people. Read the directions.

1. On your own: Think of a famous person from the past. The person can be real or fictional. Don't tell your partners.
2. Your partners take turns asking questions to guess your person.

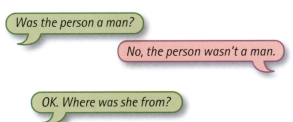

Was the person a man?

No, the person wasn't a man.

OK. Where was she from?

Frida Kahlo

 ask**&**
ANSWER

In the game in C, who was your person? Do you admire this person? Why or why not? Can you name any other heroes from the past? Why do you think they were heroes?

Heroes

Lesson B | Modern-day heroes

1 Vocabulary Link

Today's heroes

A Read about three of today's heroes. Pay attention to the words in blue.

Three Modern-day Heroes

Name: Bono   **From:** Dublin, Ireland
Occupation(s): **Musician.** He is a singer and songwriter with the band U2.
Activist. He helps the poor and homeless, and works for world peace.

Name: Arundhati Roy   **From:** Kerala, India
Occupation(s): **Novelist.** She is best known for her book *The God of Small Things.*
Activist for peace. She often speaks against war and violence.

Name: Oprah Winfrey   **From:** Mississippi, U.S.A.
Occupation(s): **talk-show host,** actress and businesswoman
Every year, Winfrey **donates** millions of dollars to help people. She gives to **charities.** These charities help children, students, the sick, and the poor all over the world.

B Match each word on the left with its definition on the right. Write the letter.

1. musician   _e_   a. this person interviews people, usually on TV or radio
2. activist   _____   b. to give something (e.g., money) to help others
3. novelist   _____   c. this person works for social change
4. peace   _____   d. freedom from violence or war
5. talk-show host   _____   e. this person plays a musical instrument
6. donate   _____   f. a company or group that helps people
7. charity   _____   g. this person writes books

ask **&**
ANSWER

Do you think the people in A are heroes? Why or why not? How are they different from the heroes in Lesson 8A? Can anyone be a hero?

2 Listening

At the zoo

  Listen. What are the man and little girl talking about? Circle the correct answer. (CD 2, Track 13)

    a. the story of Tarzan

    b. a kind gorilla

    c. a scary movie

  Listen again. Circle the correct answers. (CD 2, Track 14)

    1. At the zoo, a gorilla jumped out of its cage / a boy fell into a gorilla cage.

    2. The boy was / wasn't hurt.

    3. A woman / gorilla saved the boy.

ask & ANSWER

What stories do you know, real or imaginary, about animal heroes?

3 Reading

Making a difference

What do you know about these places: Kosovo, Afghanistan, and Chechnya?

 Read the article on page 87. Then put the events in order from 1–5.

    _____ Sierra returned to Japan and started Artists Without Borders.

    _____ Hector Sierra moved from Colombia to Japan to study film.

    _____ Sierra visited Afghanistan and Chechnya.

    _____ Sierra visited Kosovo to make a movie about the war there.

    _____ Sierra returned to Kosovo and started working with children.

B Read the article again. Then read the sentence and circle *True* or *False*. If a sentence is false, make it true.

1. Sierra started Artists Without Borders to help children in Kosovo.	True	False
2. Today, Artists Without Borders brings art to children in Japan.	True	False
3. Sierra works with children on two main projects—drawing and singing.	True	False
4. Sierra wants children to learn about other cultures.	True	False

Making a difference

Hector Sierra, a native of Colombia, is talking with a group of news reporters about his organization, Artists Without Borders. One reporter asks, "What exactly *is* AWB?" Sierra thinks for a moment, and then says, "I guess Artists Without Borders is a Colombian guy teaching Japanese culture to kids around the world . . ."

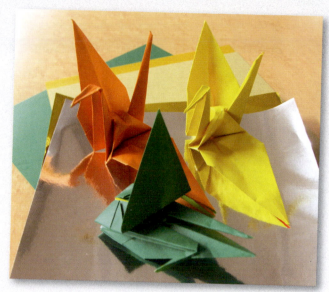

The story of Artists Without Borders begins in Tokyo in the mid-1990s. At the time, Sierra was a graduate student in film at Nihon University. As a student, Sierra visited Kosovo. He wanted to make a movie about the war there. The war made Sierra very sad. He wanted to help the people—especially the children of the area.

Sierra returned to Japan and started Artists Without Borders. He wanted to bring some happiness to the children of Kosovo, using art. Three months later, Sierra was back in Kosovo with crayons, origami paper, and paints. He started working with the children.

Since then, Artists Without Borders has visited other troubled places, including Chechnya and Afghanistan. In each place, Sierra works with children on two main projects—drawing and origami. With drawing, the kids can show their hopes and fears. With origami, the children learn to make their own toys.

Sierra wants all of the projects to be fun. But he also hopes the children learn about another culture. This, he believes, is a first step toward world peace.

ask & ANSWER

Do you think Hector Sierra is a hero? Why or why not?

World Link

Doctors Without Borders is a volunteer group started in 1971. It now offers free medical help in more than 80 countries worldwide.

A Say the sentences and words in the chart with your teacher. Pay attention to the verb forms.

Simple past: regular verbs		
I You visited Alicia didn't visit Our friends	Mexico last month.	move → moved visit → visited play → played study → studied stop → stopped

B Complete Alec's story with the simple past tense form of the verbs. Pay attention to spelling.

Help from a Stranger

There was a girl named Alyssa in my class. I (1. like) _liked_ her a lot. One day, I (2. invite) _invited_ her to have dinner with me at a nice restaurant.

After dessert, I (3. ask) _asked_ for the check. I (4. offer) _offered_ to pay. I (5. look) _looked_ in my wallet. I only had ten dollars. I (6. not have) _didn't have_ enough money!

I went to the men's room. I (7. try) _tried_ to call my roommate. I (8. wait) _waited_, but he (9. not answer) _didn't answer_ the phone. I left a message, and (10. explain) _explained_ the situation.

Just then, a bathroom door (11. open) _opened_. It was my waiter. He (12. hand) _handed_ me $20. I (13. promise) _promised_ to pay him back. He (14. reply) _replied_, "Don't worry about it."

ask&
ANSWER
Talk about a time someone helped you. What happened?

C **Pair work.** Check your answers with a partner. Then take turns reading the story aloud.

5 Writing

My hero

 Read the paragraph. Then write about your hero on a separate piece of paper.

 Share your writing with a partner. Ask your partner questions about his or her hero.

My hero is my grandmother. She was a great woman. When she was 35, she moved to the United States from Korea. At first, she didn't speak much English, but she studied hard and learned quickly. When she was 46, she started her own business. She was very smart!

My grandmother died five years ago, but I still admire her. She was a very brave and strong woman. She was a hero.

6 Communication

Hero of the Year

 Every year, your city gives a Hero of the Year award to one person. This year, there are three choices. Read about each person. Who is your choice? Why?

Carson McClure, age 30
Carson McClure is a successful businessman. This year, he donated $1,000,000 to a charity. The money is going to help 50 kids go to college.

Amanda Conrey, 54
On the night of June 24, Amanda Conrey heard a loud explosion. In front of her house, a car was on fire. A child was in the car. Amanda pulled the child out of the car. She saved the little boy's life.

Logan Myers, 22
When he was 16, Logan was in a car accident. Now, he is in a wheelchair. This year, he climbed 3,776 meters to the top of Mount Fuji using special ropes. "It was very difficult," says Myers, "but I finished the climb a day early. I'm very proud."

 Group work. Get into a group of three or four people. Explain your choice to the group.

 Group work. As a group, choose one person to get the award. Explain your answer to the class.

 Check out the World Link video. **Practice your English online at** http://elt.thomson.com/worldlink

1 Vocabulary Link

College reunion

A These people are at a college reunion. Read what the people are saying. Pay attention to the words in blue.

1. Hey, do you know this song? It reminds me of our senior year. It was really popular then.
2. A: Hi, Sherry. Do you remember me?
   B: Yes, I know your face, but I forgot your name. Is it Bill? I'm sorry, I have a bad memory.
3. In my junior year, I studied in Vienna. I have great memories of that time. I did so many fun things.
4. In Professor Smith's class, we memorized a lot of poems. I still know them.
5. Is that Jared Grant? I don't believe it! He was so thin in college!

CLASS of 1994 Ten Year Reunion

B Complete the sentences with words in blue from A. Use the correct form of the words.

1. A: Mary, what was the name of the movie on TV last night?
   B: Uhm . . . I don't _____.
2. Simon never tells the truth. You can't _____ him.
3. The best way to learn these verbs is to _____ them.
4. My phone number is 555-0978. Please write it down so you don't _____ it.
5. Naomi can look at a list of words and remember them all. She has a wonderful _____.
6. Your perfume _____ me of my sister. She wears Chanel No. 5, too.
7. I have many happy childhood _____.

ask**&**
ANSWER

Do you have a good or bad memory? Do you usually remember or forget things?
Talk about a happy high school or college memory. When was the event? What happened?
Do you have a favorite song from the past? Does it remind you of a person or place?

2 Listening

Study tips

 A Listen to Manolo and Galina talking about how they learn vocabulary. Then complete the sentence. Circle the correct word. (CD 2, Track 15)

It's difficult for Galina to pronounce / remember / spell words in English.

 B Listen to the rest of the conversation. Manolo gives Galina some study tips. Look at the pictures. Check (✓) the things Manolo does. (CD 2, Track 16)

ask**&**
ANSWER
How do you remember new vocabulary in English?

3 Pronunciation

The past tense -ed ending

 A Listen to and say the words in the chart. Pay attention to the pronunciation of the -ed ending. (CD 2, Track 17)

/t/	/d/	/ɪd/
watched	studied	waited
wished	explained	handed

 B Listen. What is the final sound of each underlined verb? Check the boxes. (CD 2, Track 18)

	/t/	/d/	/ɪd/			/t/	/d/	/ɪd/
1. I liked the movie.	✓				7. We enjoyed the visit.			✓
2. They moved to Tokyo.	✓	✓			8. Nobody believed us.			
3. It started to rain.			✓		9. Dad stopped at a store.			
4. She reminded me of you.		✓			10. We asked directions.	✓		
5. Grandma hugged us.					11. They memorized the song.			
6. We laughed loudly.	✓				12. I hated math class.			✓

A Listen to the conversation. What are Mia and Justin looking for? Where are they? (CD 2, Track 19)

Mia:	Come on, Justin. Let's go. The concert starts in an hour.
Justin:	OK, I'm coming.
Mia:	Do you have the tickets?
Justin:	Yes, they're here in my jacket. Oh, wait a minute.
Mia:	What's wrong?
Justin:	I can't find the tickets. They're not in my pocket.
Mia:	Oh no! Where are they? Are they in the desk?
Justin:	I don't think so.
Mia:	Try to remember. Maybe they're in your backpack.
Justin:	Wait . . . I found them. They were in my *other* jacket. Let's go.

B Pair work. Practice the conversation with a partner.

C Pair work. Take turns asking and answering the questions with a partner. Use the Useful Expressions to answer.

> Is the teacher from North America?

> I think so. I think she's from Canada.

1. Is your teacher from North America?
2. Is there a vending machine in your school?
3. Are there restrooms on your floor?
4. Does your partner smoke?
5. Are there restaurants near your school?
6. Is there a bus stop near your school?
7. Is your teacher a vegetarian?
8. Does your partner like pop music?

Useful Expressions:
Expressing degrees of certainty

Are the tickets in your desk?

Yes, they are.	very certain
No, they aren't.	
I think so.	
I don't think so.	
Maybe. I'm not sure.	
I have no idea.	not certain

D Look again at the picture on page 90. Study it for ten seconds. Then turn back to this page.

Whun , Where , what , whay

E Pair work. Now ask and answer the questions below with your partner. Who remembers more?

1. Are the people at their twenty-year college reunion?
2. Is there a band playing at the reunion?
3. Are there six men in the picture?
4. Is there a professor in the picture?
5. Is there a bottle on the table?
6. Are there two people holding plates?

A Study the sentences in the chart. Pay attention to the verb forms.

Simple past: irregular verbs	
I Carlos My parents	**forgot** the tickets at home. **didn't forget** the tickets at home.

B **Pair work.** What are the past forms of these verbs? Work together with a partner to write the answers. Check your answers on page 151.

1. begin   __began__
2. come   __came__
3. do   __did__
4. fall   __fell__
5. feel   __felt__

6. go   __went__
7. have   __had__
8. know   __knew__
9. make   __made__
10. run   __ran__

11. say   __saied__
12. shake   __shook__
13. think   __thought__

C Complete the story below with the past form of the verbs in parentheses. Some verbs are regular and some are irregular.

An Unforgettable Night
By Andy Liu

When I (1. be) __was__ in high school, there (2. be) __were__
a terrible earthquake in Taiwan. I will always remember that day.
It (3. begin) __began__ on September 21, 1999, early in the morning.
At 2:00 a.m., I (4. be) __was__ in bed. Suddenly,
I (5. feel) __felt__ my bed move. Just then, my brother (6. come)
__came__ into my room and (7. yell) _____, "It's an earthquake!"
The room (8. shake) __shook__ very hard. I (9. not know) __didn't know__ what to do.
I (10. run) __ran__ under a table. Books (11. fall) __fell__ from the shelves.
After about half a minute, the shaking (12. stop) __stop__. My brother and I
(13. not say) __didn't say__ anything. We (14. go) __went__ into the kitchen. There
(15. be) __were__ glass everywhere. I (16. turn on) __turn on__ the radio. The announcer
(17. say) __saied__, "A 7.6 earthquake hits Taiwan!"

D **Pair work.** Take turns reading the story in C with a partner. Then, explain the story in your own words.

Is there a day you will always remember? What happened on that day? Tell the story to a partner.

6 Communication

Early memories

 A What are some of your childhood memories?
Make notes about your ideas in the chart.

A memory about . . .	Notes
my house	
my parents	
my brothers or sisters	
my grandparents	
food	
my friends	
my toys	
music	
school	
a vacation	

 B **Pair work.** Get together with a partner. Take turns telling each other your memories.

As a child, I lived with my family in a small apartment. The apartment had a big yard. I played there with my sister . . .

C **Pair work.** Discuss the questions with your partner.

1. Are any of your memories similar to your partner's?
2. Which memory is your favorite?

D **Pair work.** Share your partner's favorite memory with the class.

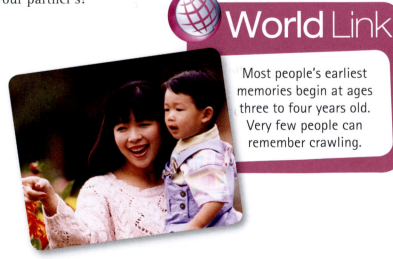

World Link

Most people's earliest memories begin at ages three to four years old. Very few people can remember crawling.

The Mind

Lesson B | In your dreams

1 Vocabulary Link

Sweet dreams!

A Study the pictures and read the sentences. Pay attention to the words in blue.

Jose is asleep. He's dreaming.
His wife is awake. She's reading.

Nadia is having a nightmare.
Her sister is saying, "Wake up!"

Marisa is daydreaming in class.

Some people study dreams.
They think dreams have special
messages or information.

Many dreams are strange and
confusing. They are hard to
understand.

What are your thoughts about
dreams? Do you have an
opinion?

B Match each word on the left with its definition. Write the letter.

1. __d__ awake   a. to stop sleeping
2. _____ asleep   b. an idea or opinion about something
3. _____ wake up   c. hard to understand
4. _____ thought   d. not sleeping
5. _____ nightmare   e. sleeping
6. _____ daydream   f. the main idea or meaning of something
7. _____ confusing   g. to think happy thoughts while awake
8. _____ message   h. a scary dream

 ANSWER

Do you usually remember your dreams? Do you think dreams have special
messages for us? Why or why not? Do you ever daydream? What about?

2 Listening

It was only a dream.

 Listen. Three people are describing their dreams. Number the pictures as you listen. (CD 2, Track 20)

 Listen again. What was strange about each person's dream? Complete the sentences. (CD 2, Track 21)

1. In class, no one / everyone / the teacher looked at Simon.
2. The dog ran toward Jesse, but Jesse wasn't scared / couldn't run / woke up.
3. Tim doesn't like fish / is afraid of the water / can't swim.

 Pair work. Use the pictures in A and your answers in B to describe each dream with a partner.

ask &
ANSWER

In your dreams, do you have special abilities?
For example, can you fly or speak another language?

 **World Link**

According to Korean folklore, if you dream about a pig, good fortune will come your way.

 3 Reading

The meaning of dreams

Do you ever try to understand the meaning of your dreams?

 How much do you know about dreams? Complete each sentence by circling the correct answer.

1. Humans usually dream only once / many times a night.
2. We often remember / don't remember all of our dreams.
3. When we dream, our brains are very active / resting.
4. The ancient Egyptians / Greeks and Romans studied dreams to help sick people.
5. Today, many scientists think dreams are meaningless / can tell us about our daily lives.

 Read the article on page 97. Were your answers in A correct?

The Meaning of *Dreams*

For centuries, people have asked: Why do we dream? What do our dreams mean? Today, science doesn't have definite answers to these questions, but we do know some things about dreams. First, we all dream, often four to five times a night. Second, we don't usually remember most of our dreams. And finally, when we dream, our brains are very active.

Thousands of years ago, people began to study dreams. In many cultures, people believed dreams were messages from spirits or gods. Later, the ancient Greeks and Romans had a new idea: Dreams come from a person's mind. Doctors studied dreams to help sick or worried people.

In the past, some cultures used dreams to predict the future. They thought dreams could help a person choose a husband or wife, guess a baby's birthday, or start a business. In some places, this practice is still common.

Today, scientists think dreams are about our thoughts and feelings. Our minds send us messages about our lives. Unfortunately, many messages are often strange or confusing. People wake up and think: What did that dream mean?

So, how can you understand the messages in your dreams? Think about the events in the dream. What do they say about *your* life? For example, one common dream is about flying. Sometimes this dream means you feel free or want freedom. Other times it means you feel afraid. What do your dreams tell you about your life?

 Read the sentences. Circle *True* or *False* according to the reading.

1.	Thousands of years ago, people believed dreams were messages from gods.	True	False
2.	In some cultures, people use dreams to predict the future.	True	False
3.	Scientists believe dreams are about your past and future.	True	False
4.	A dream about flying usually means you are tired.	True	False

ask&
ANSWER

Do you think dreams can predict the future? Why or why not? Around the world, many people have dreams about these things: water, money, flying, and falling. Do you ever have these kinds of dreams? What happens in your dream? What do you think your dream means?

4 Language Link

The simple past: question forms

A Study the chart. Then complete the conversation below with the correct past tense questions and answers. Use the words in parentheses.

	Yes/No questions	Answers	Wh-Questions	Answers
Regular verbs	**Did you study** for the test?	Yes, I did. No, I didn't.	**When did** you study?	Last night.
Irregular verbs	**Did you forget** the tickets?		**Where did** you forget the tickets?	At home.

Jay: Hey, Mario. (1. you/go) <u>Did you go</u> to the movies last night?

Mario: No, (2.) <u>I didn't</u>. I rented a movie, instead.

Jay: Oh? What (3. you/rent) <u>did you rent</u>?

Mario: The movie *28 Days Later.*

Jay: (4. you/like) <u>did you like</u> it?

Mario: Yes, (5.) <u>I did</u>, but after watching it, I (6. have) <u>had</u> nightmares.

Jay: Why (7. you/have) <u>did you have</u> nightmares?

Mario: Because it was a really scary movie. So, what (8. you/do) <u>did you do</u> last night?

Jay: I (9. go) <u>went</u> to a party with some friends.

Mario: Who (10. you/go) <u>did you go</u> with?

Jay: Margo and Antonia.

Mario: (11. you/have) <u>did you have</u> fun?

Jay: Yeah. We (12. have) <u>had</u> a great time.

B Pair work. Practice the conversation in A with a partner.

C Group work: A truth and a lie. Read the directions to do this activity.

1. Get into a group of three or four people. Tell the group two things: something you really did, and something you didn't really do. Use one sentence for each.

2. Your group members ask you questions about both activities. They guess which activity is true and which is a lie.

When I was a child, I lived in Paris.

Really? Why did you live in Paris?

5 Writing

A strange dream

A Read the paragraph on the right. What do you think this dream means?

Two days ago, I had a strange dream. I was on a beach. It was a warm, sunny day, and I was very happy. Suddenly, the weather changed. It started to rain. I was very afraid. I yelled for help. And then, I woke up.

B Pair work. Exchange papers with a partner. Ask your partner a question about his or her dream.

6 Communication

The house in my dream

 A Pair work. Follow the instructions below.

Student A: Your partner is going to read to you. Listen. Write notes in the chart.

Places in the house	Notes
The outside of the house	
The living room	
The kitchen	
The bedroom	

Student B: Read the text below to your partner. Read slowly.

- Imagine that you are asleep. You are having a dream about your ideal house. Imagine that you are standing outside your house. Look at it. What does it look like? What color is the house? How big is it?
- Now you are in the house. You walk into your living room. What does it look like? How do you feel in this room?
- Next, you are in the kitchen. What does it look like? Is anything happening in the kitchen?
- Finally, you are in your bedroom. What does it look like? How do you feel in this room?

B Pair work. Switch roles and repeat activity A.

C Pair work. Talk about your "dream house" with your partner.

Student A: Describe your house.
Student B: What does your partner's "dream" mean? Use the information below to talk about the meaning.

The outside of the house:	This is your personality.
The living room:	This room shows your feelings about other people.
The kitchen:	This room shows your hopes for the future.
The bedroom:	This room shows your feelings about love.

D Pair work. Switch roles and repeat activity C.

> What did your house look like?

> My house was light blue. The house wasn't big, but it had a lot of windows. I like light.

> Hmmm . . . your house had a lot of windows. Maybe you are an outgoing and friendly person.

 Check out the World Link video. **Practice your English online at http://elt.thomson.com/worldlink**

1 Storyboard

 Pair work. Vivian and Jun are visiting a museum. Look at the pictures and work with a partner to complete the conversations. More than one answer is possible for each blank.

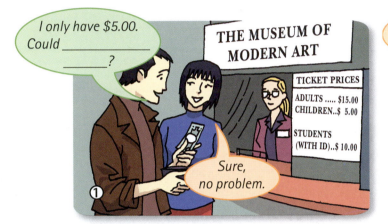

B **Pair work.** Practice the conversation with a partner. Then switch roles and practice again.

A **Pair work.** Talk about the picture.

- Where are these people?
- What are they doing?
- Look at the different ads. What are they about?
- Ask one more question about the picture.
- Do you take publice transportation often?
  How is it? Clean? Safe? Inexpensive? Crowded?

B **Pair work.** Choose one pair of people in the picture. Role-play a conversation between the two people.

3 Who are we going to invite?

 A You are going to have a dinner party. You can invite four famous people from the past or the present. Complete the chart with the names of the people you want to invite. List your reasons for inviting them.

1. Person:	
Reason:	
2. Person:	
Reason:	
3. Person:	
Reason:	
4. Person:	
Reason:	

B **Group work.** Get into a group of three people. Compare your answers in A. Explain your choices. Together, make one list of four people to invite to the party.

I think we should invite Bob Marley. He was a great musician and a peace activist.

Yeah, I agree. Let's invite him.

4 Listening: Summer vacation

  A Jim and Hal are college roommates. Listen. What are they talking about? Complete the sentence below. (CD 2, Track 22)

Jim and Hal are talking about _____.

    a. summer plans

    b. summer school

    c. a summer home

  B Listen again. Read the sentences and write *J* for Jim or *H* for Hal. (CD 2, Track 23)

_____ is going home.

_____ is going to get a job.

_____ is going to his sister's home.

_____ is going to rest.

_____ is planning to be in Toronto in July.

 C **Pair work.** Ask your partner: Do you have plans for the summer? What are you going to do?

A **Pair work.** Look at the wedding announcement below. Two people are getting married. Think of a man and a woman. They can be famous people or other people you know. Complete the information about them.

THEY'RE GETTING MARRIED!

Name:
Occupation:
Age:
Where from:

Name:
Occupation:
Age:
Where from:

B Work alone. You are going to interview these people.
Look at the questions and think of three more to ask the couple.

- When did you meet?
- How did you meet?
- When are you going to get married?
- Who are you going to invite to the wedding?
- _____?
- _____?
- _____?

C **Pair work. Role play.** The interview.

Partner A: You are one of the people in A. Answer the reporter's questions. Use your imagination.
Partner B: You are a newspaper reporter. Use your questions to interview the man or woman. Take notes.

D **Pair work.** Switch roles and do activity C again.

E **Group work.** Share some of your interview notes with another pair.

I interviewed Prince William. He's dating Mia, our classmate! They're going to get married next month!

Really? How did they meet?

10 Your Health

Lesson A | Health and body

1 Vocabulary Link

Touch your toes!

A Match the words in the boxes with a part of the body in the pictures.

Head and shoulders

a. eye
b. tooth *(pl. = teeth)*
c. nose
d. ear
e. mouth
f. neck
g. shoulder
h. head

Parts of the body

1. arm
2. hand
3. finger
4. chest
5. stomach
6. leg
7. ankle
8. foot *(pl. = feet)*
9. toe

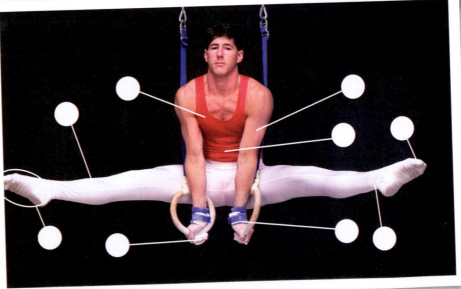

B **Pair work.** Complete the sentence with a part of the body. Say the sentence to your partner. Your partner does the action. Take turns doing this five times each.

Touch your . . . !

Touch your toes!

Wanted!

 A Mrs. Wilkins saw a robbery last night. She is describing the robber to a police officer. Listen. Check (✓) the picture of the robber. (CD 2, Track 24)

 B Listen again. Circle the correct word to complete each sentence. (CD 2, Track 25)

1. The robber is about 21 / 29 years old.
2. The robber is / isn't tall.
3. The robber has a tattoo on his back / hand.

 C Pair work. Close your book. Describe the robber to your partner.

World Link

Perhaps the most heavily tattooed culture in history was a tribe from the Visayas islands in the Philippines. The Spanish explorers who met them in the 1500s called them "pintados", meaning "the painted ones".

3 Pronunciation

Reduced *h*

 A Listen to the conversation below. Pay attention to the underlined words. Notice how the *h* sound disappears. (CD 2, Track 26)

A: Where's your brother?
B: He's in bed.
A: Is he sick?

B: Yes, he is.
A: Here. Give him some aspirin.

B Read the conversation below. Cross out the *h* in each underlined pronoun. The first one has been done for you.

Man: Captain, this is Mrs. Mitchell. A man stole her purse.
Captain: OK, Mrs. Mitchell. Tell me about him. Was he tall?
Woman: Yes, he was.
Captain: What else?

Woman: Well, I saw a tattoo.
Captain: Where?
Woman: On his right arm.

 C Listen to the conversation. Pay attention to the pronunciation of the underlined words. (CD 2, Track 27)

 D Pair work. Practice the conversations in A and B with a partner.

4 Speaking

I don't feel well.

 A Listen to the conversation. What's wrong with Jon? (CD 2, Track 28)

Chloe: Hello?

Jon: Hi, Chloe. It's Jon.

Chloe: Jon! Where are you? It's 7:30.
The movie starts in twenty minutes.

Jon: Sorry to call so late, but I can't meet
you tonight.

Chloe: Really?

Jon: Yeah, I don't feel well.

Chloe: What's wrong?

Jon: I have a headache, and I'm really tired.

Chloe: Oh, sorry to hear that. Well, get some rest, and I'll call you in the morning.

Jon: OK. Talk to you then.

B **Pair work.** Practice the conversation with a partner.

C **Pair work.** What's wrong with Jon? Say sentences about the pictures to your partner.

He has a(n) . . .

| earache | stomachache | sore throat | cough | fever |

D **Pair work.** Take turns practicing the conversation in A again. Use the words from C in the conversation.

E **Pair work. Role play.** You have plans to meet a friend, but you don't feel well. Call your friend and explain the situation. Use the Useful Expressions to help you.

F **Pair work.** Change roles and practice again.

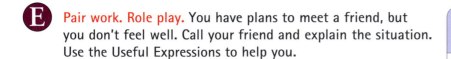

Hi, Maria. It's Vlad. Sorry, but I don't feel well.

> **Useful Expressions:**
> **Talking about health problems**
>
> What's wrong?/What's the matter?
>   I don't feel well.
>   I'm sick.
>   I have a/an . . .
>   My . . . hurts.

Study the sentences in the pictures. Notice the use of the imperative in the words in blue. Then, complete the sentences below.

Relax for an hour. You're tired. Don't work so hard.

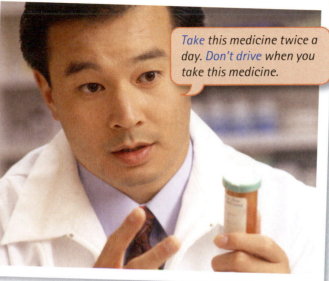

Take this medicine twice a day. Don't drive when you take this medicine.

1. In an imperative statement, the subject is always *you*, but we say / don't say it.

2. Circle all the correct answers. Use the imperative to give instructions / ask questions / give advice.

 Complete the following health tips with the positive or negative imperative. Use the verbs in the box. Some verbs can be used more than once.

drink	eat	give	go	sleep	take	wash

Health tips: The common cold

To stay healthy:

1. _Take_ vitamins.
2. _Don't eat_ a lot of junk food.
3. _____ for 8–9 hours a night.
4. _____ your hands often.

If you have a cold:

5. _____ to school or work.
6. _____ a lot of water and juice.
7. _____ aspirin for pain and fever.
8. _____ aspirin to children under 12! It's dangerous.

C Pair work. Take turns with your partner. Imagine that you have one of these health problems. Add one more to the list. Ask your partner for some advice.

1. I can't sleep at night.
2. I have a stomachache.
3. When I exercise, my legs hurt.
4. _____

I can't sleep at night.

Don't drink coffee in the evening!

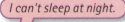

Pair work. Read the poster below. Then, answer the questions with a partner.

1. What does the poster tell people to do?
2. What other ideas can you add to the list?
3. Are there posters like this one in your city? Where?

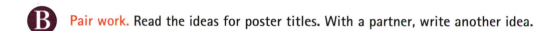

Say NO to smoking.

Stop smoking today. How can you do it?
- Choose a date to stop smoking.
- Tell your friends and family about your plan. Ask for their help.
- Talk to your doctor. Ask for help.

B Pair work. Read the ideas for poster titles. With a partner, write another idea.

Fight pollution in our city!	Eat healthy, live longer.
Get in shape today!	Protect your skin this summer!
Don't drink and drive.	Your idea: _____

C Pair work. Write one of the poster titles from B in the chart.
Think of how people can do it. List three ideas in the chart.

Poster Title: _____

How can you do it?
1. _____
2. _____
3. _____

 Pair work. On a separate piece of paper, make a poster telling people about your ideas in C.

E Group work. Present your poster to another pair. Discuss it with them.

Your Health

Lesson B | Fighting stress, staying healthy

Ask the doctor.

A Look at the pictures. Read about these students' problems. Pay attention to the words in blue.

Jeff

Nora

Sally

I'm stressed. I have a paper due on Thursday, and a test on Friday! What can I do?

I'm exhausted. I go to school and work 30 hours a week. On the weekend, I don't have any energy. I just sleep all day. Help!

I'm down. My boyfriend and I had a fight. I'm not doing well in school. What can I do?

B Pair work. Read Doctor Martino's advice. Who is her advice for? Write Jeff, Nora, or Sally. Tell your partner.

Dr. Martino's advice	For . . .
You're very unhappy. Can you talk to a teacher or friend? If not, please visit me in the Student Health Center.	
Try to be calm. Talk to your teachers about the papers. Maybe you can have more time.	
First, reduce your work hours to 15 hours a week. Also, you need to sleep more. Then, you'll feel more energetic.	

C Pair work. Discuss these questions with a partner.

1. What things cause stress?   2. How can you reduce stress?

A Listen to Brian and Lisa talking about his grandmother. Which picture is probably his grandmother? Check (✓) the picture and explain your choice to a classmate. (CD 2, Track 29)

 B Listen again. Which things are true about Brian's grandmother? Check (✓) the boxes. (CD 2, Track 30)

1. ☐ She's energetic.   ☐ Her memory isn't very good.

2. ☐ She eats a lot of sugar and salt.   ☐ She has a good diet.

3. ☐ She exercises once in a while.   ☐ She exercises every day.

4. ☐ She's a piano teacher.   ☐ She doesn't read much.

 C **Pair work.** Compare your answers in B with a partner.

ask **&**
ANSWER
Who is the oldest person in your family?
How old is he or she? How is his/her health?

3 Reading

Exam stress: What can I do?

> Do you think taking tests is stressful? Explain your answer with an example.

 A Read the letter from *Sleepless in Seoul* on page 111. What is the writer's problem?

a. The writer has too much schoolwork.

b. The writer is worried about a test.

c. The writer failed an exam last Friday.

B Read Donna's answer. At the beginning of each tip from Donna,
write the correct introductory sentence from this box.

> Eat well.   Take breaks and relax.   Get a study partner.   Don't do too much.

Dear Donna

Problems? Just ask Donna.

Dear Donna,

Help! I'm an 18-year-old high school student in Seoul. In eight months, I'm going to take the university entrance exam. To prepare, I'm studying six hours a day. I want to do well, but I'm really stressed these days. I can't sleep. What can I do?

Signed,
Sleepless in Seoul

Dear Sleepless,

Your problem is a common one for many students around the world. Here are some tips to help you.

Good luck!

1. _____ Make a study schedule for yourself, but don't study too much in one day. You remember more by studying one hour each day for six days, than six hours in one day. Also, don't study late at night (we often forget information studied then).

2. _____ You learn best when you study in two hour blocks. Every two hours, take a break for 15 to 20 minutes. Go outside and walk. Exercise is a great way to reduce stress. It can also improve memory and help you sleep better at night.

3. _____ Don't eat or drink a lot of sugar and caffeine. Eat foods high in vitamin B (for example, eggs, yogurt, green vegetables, tofu, rice). These give you energy and help you think more clearly.

4. _____ A study partner can help you practice for the test. When you're worried about the exam, you can talk to your partner. This can reduce stress, too.

 C Complete each sentence. Circle the correct words.

1. The student is stressed about taking an important test on Friday / in eight months.
2. Donna thinks it's better to study a lot one day / a little each day.
3. We often remember / forget information when we study late at night.
4. When you study, it's good to take a break every 20 minutes / 2 hours.
5. Foods and drinks high in sugar and caffeine / vitamin B give you energy and help you think more clearly.
6. Thinking / Talking about your worries can help reduce stress.

ask& ANSWER

The reading lists four ways to reduce study stress. Can you think of other ways? What was the last test you took? Was it hard? How did you prepare?

4 Language Link

When-clauses

> The result can come first in a sentence:
> I cry when I see sad movies.

A Study the sentences in the chart.

When-clause	Result clause	
When(ever) I drink a lot of coffee,	I can't sleep.	These sentences mean *When X happens, Y is the result.*
When(ever) I see sad movies,	I cry.	

B Match a *when*-clause on the left with a result clause on the right to make sentences.

1. When I feel stressed,
2. When we argue,
3. When I sleep well,
4. When I don't eat breakfast,
5. When you're kind,
6. When I miss the bus

a. people are usually nice to you.
b. I get hungry by 10:00.
c. my mom usually apologizes first.
d. I exercise.
e. I'm usually late for class.
f. I have a lot of energy the next day.

C **Pair work.** Rewrite the sentences in B so that the result is first. Then tell your partner which sentences are true for you. Explain your answers.

1. I exercise when I feel stressed.
2. _____
3. _____
4. _____
5. _____
6. _____

D Complete the sentences with your own information.

1. When I don't feel well, I take aspirin and drink tea _____.
2. When I meet new people, _____.
3. When I don't understand something in English, _____.
4. I feel stressed when _____.
5. I feel _____ when _____.

E **Pair work.** Take turns saying the sentences in D. For each sentence, your partner asks you one question.

> When I don't feel well, I take aspirin and drink tea.

> Really? What kind of tea?

World Link

It is predicted that by 2020, five of the top ten medical problems worldwide will be stress-related.

5 Writing

A remedy for stress

 A When you feel stressed, what do you do? Read the paragraph about Dmitri. Then write about your ideas on a separate piece of paper.

I'm a college senior. Next semester, I'm going to graduate. A lot of things in my life are going to change. Sometimes, I feel stressed. What do I do? I try to be calm. Whenever I feel really worried, I talk to my friend Sergei. We talk about our future plans. That helps a lot!

Dmitri, Moscow

 B Pair work. Exchange your paper with a partner. Ask questions about your partner's ideas.

6 Communication

Stress survey

 A Pair work. Interview your partner. Check (✓) the answer that describes him or her.

Stress Survey

1. When you have to wait in a line, do you usually
- ☐ get nervous and impatient?
- ☐ wait patiently?
- ☐ other: _____

2. When you have a lot to do, do you usually
- ☐ wait until the last day and do everything?
- ☐ make a schedule and do some work everyday?
- ☐ other: _____

3. When you have some free time, do you usually
- ☐ find something to do?
- ☐ relax?
- ☐ other: _____

4. When you feel stressed, what do you do?
- ☐ I don't tell anyone.
- ☐ I tell a friend or family member.
- ☐ other: _____

5. When someone disagrees with you, do you
- ☐ argue with the person?
- ☐ change your opinion?
- ☐ other: _____

6. When you don't do well at something, do you
- ☐ get angry?
- ☐ feel disappointed, but don't get mad?
- ☐ other: _____

 B Pair work. Think about your partner's answers. Is your partner a calm or a stressed person? Explain your answer.

 Check out the World Link video.   **Practice your English online at** http://elt.thomson.com/worldlink

1 Vocabulary Link

Talented people

A Read about these talented people. Pay attention to the words in blue.

Garry Kasparov is from Azerbaijan. He became the world chess champion at age 22. Today, he competes against powerful computers.

David Blaine is a famous American magician. In the photo, he is doing a magic trick.

Sonya Fitzpatrick has a special talent: She can talk to animals.

Shakira is a singer from Colombia. She wrote her first song at age 8. This talented woman also speaks three languages.

Chandra Sekar, from India, is a computer wiz. He passed a Microsoft engineering test at age 10.

The artist, Leonardo da Vinci, was also an inventor. In the 1500s, he imagined airplanes, parachutes, and contact lenses!

B Match each word on the left with its definition.

_____ 1. a talent	a. very good at something
_____ 2. an inventor	b. a person who does magic
_____ 3. a champion	c. a person who can do something very, very well
_____ 4. a wiz	d. a special ability or skill
_____ 5. a magician	e. a person with ideas for new things
_____ 6. a trick	f. to try to win in a game or sport
_____ 7. talented	g. a great player, a winner
_____ 8. compete	h. part of a magic show—it looks real, but it isn't

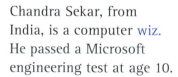

ask & ANSWER

In your opinion, who is the most talented person in A? Why?

2 Listening

She talks to animals.

communicate (v.): to give information to others, usually by speaking

 A Peter and Molly are talking about a TV show. Listen. Which picture describes the show? Circle it. (CD 2, Track 31)

 B Listen again. Circle the correct answers. (CD 2, Track 32)

1. Sonya Fitzpatrick uses her mind / special words to communicate with an animal.
2. On last week's show, Sonya met a worried / sad dog named Skippy.
3. Skippy's friend, Sam the dog, died / ran away.
4. Peter thinks the TV show is interesting / silly.

ask&
ANSWER

Do you think animals can communicate with humans? Do you know of any animals with special talents?

3 Pronunciation

Can/can't, could/couldn't

  A Listen to the sentences. Pay attention to the pronunciation of the underlined words. (CD 2, Track 33)

1. She <u>can</u> speak three languages.
2. I <u>can't</u> play the piano.
3. At age three, Maya <u>could</u> count to 1,000.
4. The movie was in French. I <u>couldn't</u> understand it.

  B Listen and circle the word you hear. (CD 2, Track 34)

1. Billy can / can't sing very well.
2. I can / can't do magic tricks.
3. I can / can't go out with you tonight.
4. Jill can / can't meet us after class.
5. Sean could / couldn't play soccer very well.
6. I could / couldn't swim as a child.
7. We could / couldn't hear the speaker.
8. Did you see Joe? He could / couldn't dance!

 C **Pair work.** Say the sentences in B to your partner. Are you saying *can* or *can't*, *could* or *couldn't*? Your partner points to the word.

4 Speaking

You can paint really well.

  A Tyler and Ayumi are at a party. Listen to the conversation. Does Tyler like Ayumi's painting? (CD 2, Track 35)

Ayumi: Hi, Tyler. Are you enjoying yourself?

Tyler: Yeah, thanks, Ayumi.

Ayumi: Do you want a drink?

Tyler: Sure, I'll have a soda. Hey, I have a question. This painting is very interesting. Who's the artist?

Ayumi: Uh . . . I am.

Tyler: Yeah? I like your work a lot.

Ayumi: Oh, it's OK. I just paint for fun.

Tyler: Well, you can paint really well.

Ayumi: Thanks. That's nice of you to say.

B **Pair work.** Practice the conversation with a partner.

C **Pair work.** With a partner, create new conversations for Situations 1 and 2 below. Use the Useful Expressions to help you.

Useful Expressions:	
Offering compliments	Accepting compliments
This/Your . . . is very interesting/ beautiful/smart. That's a nice/cool . . . I like this/your . . . a lot. You can . . . really well.	Thank you. Thanks. That's nice of you to say.

Situation 1	Situation 2
Student A: You're a guitarist. You wrote a new song and you're practicing it. **Student B:** You hear your partner practicing a song. You like it. You think your partner plays well.	**Student B:** You're wearing a new sweater. It didn't cost a lot of money. **Student A:** Your partner is wearing a new sweater. You think it's cool.

ask&
ANSWER
How often do you compliment others?

Is it OK to compliment an older person? Why or why not?

How about complimenting a person of the opposite sex?

5 Language Link

Talking about skills and talents with *can* and *could*

 Pair work. Study the chart. Then complete the sentences below.

Talking about skills and talents with *can* and *could*	
Can you speak Spanish?	Yes, I **can.** No, I **can't.**
Who can speak French?	Naoki **can.** My parents **can't.**
Could you speak Spanish as a child?	Yes, I **could.** No, I **couldn't.**
Who could read at age two?	Monika **could.** Jackie **couldn't.**

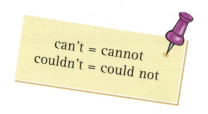

In the Suzuki method for teaching violin and piano (developed by Japanese violinist Shinichi Suzuki), students start to study at the age of four.

1. To talk about skills and talents in the present, use can / could.
2. To talk about skills and talents in the past, use can / could.

B Complete the sentences with the correct form of *can* or *could.*

1. Jared is a language wiz. He _____ speak five languages fluently.
2. Ajay Puri was a very talented child. When he was four, he _____ build websites.
3. Satoshi Fukushima is a professor at Tokyo University. The interesting thing is—he _____ hear or see.
4. Valentina _____ count to 100 when she was three.
5. Sonya _____ understand pets on her show, but the animals _____ actually speak to her.
6. For years, my grandmother _____ use a computer. Then she took a class. Now she _____ send e-mail, surf the Web, and shop online.

C **Class activity.** Add your own question to the chart. Then find a classmate who answers *Yes* for each question. Write the classmate's name. Then the classmate performs the action for you.

Can you . . .	Classmate's name
1. sing a song in English?	
2. draw well?	
3. dance well?	
4. say "I love you" in three languages?	
5.	

Can you sing a song in English?

Yes. I can sing "Happy Birthday."

ask & ANSWER

What is something you can do now but couldn't do in the past? How did you learn to do it?

6 Communication

Talent search!

 A Read about the TV show *Talent Search!*
Do you know any other shows like this one?

> *Talent Search!* is a popular TV show. Talented people compete against each other for prizes. Some people sing or dance. Others tell jokes, do magic tricks, or act. The audience chooses the best person.

B Imagine that you are going to be on Talent Search! Complete the form about yourself.

> 1. Name: _____
>
> 2. Where from: _____
>
> 3. What is your special talent? Explain your talent.
>
> 4. What are you going to do on the show? Explain your idea.

C Pair work. Get together with a partner and ask him or her questions to complete the form in B. Write the answers on a separate piece of paper.

> *What is your special talent?*

> *Well, I can sing and dance well . . .*

D Group work. You and your partner should join two other pairs. Imagine that you are a *Talent Search!* announcer. Introduce your partner to the group. Use your notes from C.

E Group work.
Who has the most interesting talent in your group? Why?

> *Presenting a talented young woman from Mexico City— Marina Perez! She can . . .*

That's Amazing

Lesson B | Amazing achievements

1 Vocabulary Link

Special achievements

A Read about these people's special achievements. Pay attention to the words in blue.

Special achievements

A Vietnamese restaurant

The Zapp family

Robert David Hall

Diana An is an amazing business-woman. She opened one of the first Vietnamese restaurants in San Francisco. Today, she also owns restaurants in Beverly Hills and Las Vegas. What's her advice? "Be confident," she says. "Tell yourself 'I can do it.'"

Herman and Candelaria Zapp had a dream—to visit Alaska. They drove 40,000 miles (64,373 km) from Buenos Aires, Argen-tina to Anchorage, Alaska. They had very little money, and the journey took over three years. But they did it!

At age 31, actor Robert David Hall was in a car accident. He survived, but he lost his legs. Life was difficult, but Hall didn't give up. He continued to work. Today, he is a successful actor in Hollywood.

B Complete the sentences with the words in blue from A. Use the correct form of the words.

1. Aya is only 13 and she won an Olympic medal. What an _____!
2. It's a long _____ by car from San Francisco to New York.
3. A person can't _____ without water.
4. Mia can remember everything she reads. She has an _____ memory.
5. Marty is very shy. He isn't self-_____.
6. Come on . . . we can finish this project. Let's not _____ now!

ask&
ANSWER

In your opinion, whose achievement in A is the most amazing? Why?

A Listen. What are the man and woman talking about? Check (✓) the correct photo. (CD 2, Track 36)

  B Now listen to the rest of the conversation. Circle the correct words. (CD 2, Track 37)

1. La Quebrada cliffs are in Mexico City / Acapulco.
2. The divers are very careful. There are a lot of rocks / sharks in the water.
3. The cliffs are 45 / 55 meters high.
4. The woman saw the divers in Mexico / on television.

ask & ANSWER

Many tourists visit La Quebrada to see the divers. Name a popular tourist attraction you know.

3 Reading

Two amazing achievements

How many days can you be by yourself with nobody to talk to?

 A **Pair work.** Read the titles of the two stories on page 121 and look at the pictures. What do you think the stories are about? Tell your partner.

 B Now read the stories.

World Link

One of the world's best-known novels is Daniel Defoe's *Robinson Crusoe* (1719). The story is based on the life of sailor Alexander Selkirk, who lived alone on a small island off Chile for more than four years.

Man leaves box after 44 days

In 2003, magician David Blaine spent 44 days in a small box in London. For six weeks, Blaine didn't eat any food. He survived by drinking water. During his stay, thousands of people came to watch him. And what did they see? "I didn't see anything," said one visitor to the site. "Blaine just sat in the box. Once, he waved to us, but that was it."

So, why did Blaine sit in a box and not eat for 44 days? Eileen from London believes "He wanted the attention. He was on TV and in all the newspapers. It's great for his career!"

Richard from Vancouver has a different opinion. "Blaine didn't do any magic. Still, almost 200,000 people came to watch him sit in a box and do nothing. Now that's an amazing trick!"

Teenage sailor crosses the Atlantic

Fifteen-year-old Sebastian Clover arrived in Antigua early yesterday morning. Clover, a high school student from the UK, sailed alone across the Atlantic Ocean. Waiting to meet him at the harbor were his parents, a band of musicians, and the Governor-General of Antigua and Barbuda.

Sebastian's journey began on December 19. He sailed his boat from the Canary Islands and arrived in Antigua and Barbuda on January 12.

How was the trip? For Clover, the high point was seeing whales and dolphins. But sometimes it was frightening being alone on the boat—especially in bad weather. It was also hard to eat well. Clover usually ate snacks because it was difficult to cook.

It was an amazing trip, but Sebastian also admits he's glad to be back on land!

 Read the sentences. Who is each sentence about? Circle *David* or *Sebastian*.

1. He crossed the Atlantic by himself on a boat.	David	Sebastian
2. He ate snacks for about three weeks.	David	Sebastian
3. He didn't eat anything for over six weeks.	David	Sebastian
4. A lot of people came to see him.	David	Sebastian
5. Sometimes, he felt scared being alone.	David	Sebastian
6. He saw some interesting animals.	David	Sebastian
7. Some people think he wanted attention.	David	Sebastian

ask & ANSWER

In the David Blaine story, Eileen and Richard have different opinions. Who do you agree with? Sebastian Clover had an amazing adventure. What is something exciting you'd like to do?

4 Language Link

Connecting ideas with *because*

> The reason can also come first in a sentence:
>
> *Because I didn't eat breakfast, I'm hungry.*

A Study the sentences in the chart. Then complete the sentence below the correct answer(s).

	Main clause	Reason
Why are you hungry?	I'm hungry	**because** I didn't eat breakfast.
Why were you late?	I was late	**because** I missed the bus.
Why should I visit Japan?	You should visit Japan	**because** it's a beautiful country.

Use *because* to . . . ☐ answer the question *why?*   ☐ give a reason.

☐ ask a question.   ☐ join two sentences.

> In rapid speech, *because* is often pronounced "cuz."

B **Pair work.** Combine the sentences below using *because*. Then take turns saying them with a partner

1. The teacher is sick. There's no class today.

   _____

2. It was cold. We didn't go to the beach.

   _____

3. I had a headache. I took some aspirin.

   _____

4. It's old. You should sell your car.

   _____

5. School is closed for a month. We're going to go on vacation in January.

   _____

6. It's bad for his health. Rich shouldn't smoke.

   _____

C Complete the questions with your ideas.

1. Why is _____?
2. Why was _____?
3. Why did _____?
4. Why should(n't) _____?

D **Pair work.** Take turns asking and answering questions from C with a partner.

Why is this classroom so cold?

Because the windows are open!

5 Writing

An amazing experience

 A Read the paragraphs below. Then, write about an amazing or unusual experience of your own.

> Last summer, I went backpacking for ten days in the Rocky Mountains. First, things were hard because I wasn't in shape. Every day, we hiked 10 miles. Sometimes I thought, "Am I going to survive?"
>
> After a few days, I was more comfortable. The scenery was very beautiful.
>
> The backpacking trip wasn't easy, but it was an amazing experience!

 B **Pair work.** Exchange your writing with a partner. Ask your partner questions about his or her experience.

6 Communication

Thirteen things to do

A Look at the activities below. Which things would you like to do? Check (✓) them. Which don't you want to do? Put an X next to them.

Thirteen things to do before you're 70

- ○ learn to fly a plane
- ○ travel around the world
- ○ learn to speak three languages
- ○ get a tattoo
- ○ learn to play a musical instrument
- ○ gamble in Las Vegas or Monte Carlo
- ○ go to a game played at the Olympics or the World Cup

- ○ shave your head for a year
- ○ run in a marathon
- ○ drive an expensive car
- ○ act in a movie
- ○ go bungee jumping
- ○ send someone a love letter
- ○ Your idea: _____

 B **Pair work.** Get together with a partner and take turns comparing your answers. Explain your choices.

> *I don't want to learn to fly a plane.*

> *Really? Why not?*

> *Because it's too scary!*

 Check out the World Link video. **Practice your English online at http://elt.thomson.com/worldlink**

1 Vocabulary Link

Types of movies

A Look at the movie posters. What kinds of movies are they? Match a word in the box with a film. For some movies, more than one answer is possible.

a. action/adventure	c. science fiction (sci-fi)	e. romance	g. drama
b. animation	d. horror	f. musical	h. comedy

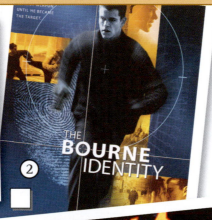

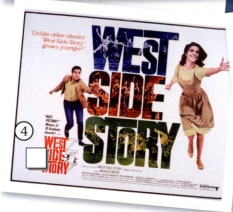

B **Pair work.** Compare your answers in A with a partner. Can you think of other movie types?

ask &
ANSWER

What kinds of movies do you like? What kinds don't you like? Why? What's your favorite movie? What kind of film is it? Do you ever watch old movies from the 1920s, '30s, or '40s?

2 Listening

What should we rent?

 A Marta and Jay are in a video store. Listen. Number the films they talk about in the order you hear them. (CD 2, Track 38)

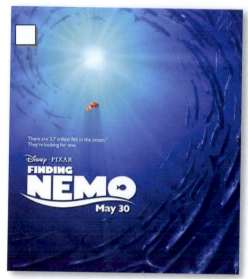

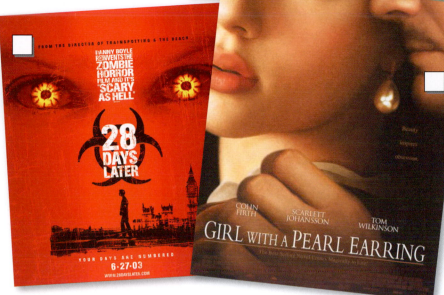

 B Listen again. Complete each sentence with the correct answer. (CD 2, Track 39)

1. Jay thinks *Girl with a Pearl Earring* is a beautiful / sad film.
2. Jay says *Finding Nemo* is a movie for kids / children and adults.
3. Marta wants / doesn't want to see *28 Days Later* because it's scary.

3 Pronunciation

Intonation in questions of choice

ask&
ANSWER

How often do you go to the movies?
What kinds of movies do you usually rent?

 A In each question below, a person is offering a choice. Notice the rising intonation in the first choice and the falling intonation in the second. (CD 2, Track 40)

[↗]   [↘]

1. What do you want to see, Chicago or Moulin Rouge?

[↗]   [↘]

2. When does the movie start, 7:00 or 7:30?

 B Listen to the questions. Draw rising [↗] and falling arrows [↘] over the correct words in each sentence. (CD 2, Track 41)

1. Which movie is Johnny Depp in, *Titanic* or *Chocolat*?
2. Where's the theater, on Seventh Avenue or Eighth?
3. What time do you want to meet, noon or 1:00?
4. How was the movie, interesting or boring?

C Pair work. Practice saying the sentences in A and B with a partner.

Can I take a message?

 A Listen to the conversation. Who is Silvio calling? Why is he calling? (CD 2, Track 42)

Pam:	Hello?
Silvio:	Hi. Is Michael there, please?
Pam:	Who's calling?
Silvio:	This is Silvio, a friend from school.
Pam:	OK. Hang on a minute.
Silvio:	Thanks.
Pam:	Hello? Sorry. Michael's not here. Can I take a message?
Silvio:	Yeah. There's an interesting movie playing tonight at the Strand Theater. It's called *Silence at Sunset*. I have two tickets.
Pam:	OK. I'll tell him.

hang on = please wait

 B Pair work. Practice the conversation with a partner.

C Write a movie you want to see, a time, a place, and a friend to invite.

Movie title	Time	Place	Friend's name

 D Pair work. Role play. With your partner, play one of these roles in a phone conversation. Use the Useful Expressions to help you.

Student A: You call your friend to invite him or her to a movie. Your friend isn't home. Leave a message with a family member.

Student B: Answer the phone. Take a message.

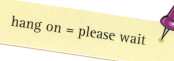
Hello? Is Hiro there?

PHONE MESSAGE
Who called: _____

Message: _____

_____

_____

Useful Expressions:
Telephoning

Hello? Is Michael there?
 Who's calling?
This is Silvio.
 OK. Hang on a minute.
 Sorry. Michael isn't here.
 Can I take a message?

 E Pair work. Switch roles and practice again.

-ing/-ed **adjectives**

 A **Pair work.** Read the sentences in the box. Pay attention to the adjectives in bold. Complete the sentences with a partner.

> I'm **bored.**
>
> This movie is **boring.** Let's watch something else.
>
> Julie is **interested** in Charlie Chaplin's movies.
> Julie thinks Charlie Chaplin was **interesting.**

1. These adjectives describe a person's emotion or feeling: _____, _____
2. These adjectives describe the cause of an emotion or feeling: _____, _____

B Complete the movie review. Choose the correct form of the adjectives.

The Two-minute Movie Review
reviewed by: Paula

Actor Haley Clarkson is in the new sci-fi thriller *Midnight on the Moon.*
Overall, I was very disappointed / disappointing with this film. I expected
a great movie, but this one was terrible!

Some scenes in the film are excited / exciting, and newcomer Kristin Ng
is interested / interesting as Clarkson's love interest in the movie. But the
story is often confusing / confused. I didn't understand the ending at all.
I was also shocked / shocking by the violence in the film. Too much blood!

If you want to see a great sci-fi thriller, don't see *Midnight on the Moon.*
I was bored / boring. My advice: See the 1982 classic *Blade Runner.* It's
in theaters for a month. It's an amazed / amazing sci-fi movie!

 C **Pair work.** Take turns reading the paragraphs of
the movie review in B aloud with a partner.

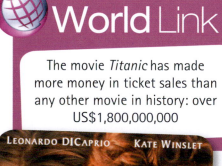

World Link

The movie *Titanic* has made
more money in ticket sales than
any other movie in history: over
US$1,800,000,000

D **Pair work.** Choose adjectives from B to complete the sentences.
Then use the sentences to interview a partner.

1. Tell me about a(n) _____ experience.
2. When was the last time you were _____?
3. Talk about a(n) _____ movie you saw.

A What was the last movie you saw in a movie theater, on video, DVD, or TV? Complete the chart with your information.

	Me	Partner 1	Partner 2
What was the last movie you saw?			
What type of film was it?			
Who was in the movie?			
Use two adjectives to describe the movie.			
Did you like the movie? Why or why not?			

B **Class activity.** Interview two classmates using the questions in A. Write their answers in the chart.

> *What was the last movie you saw?*

> *The last movie I saw was Whale Rider . . .*

Whale Rider

C **Group work.** Get into a group of two or three people you did not interview in B. Talk about the movies in your charts. Which one(s) do you want to see? Why?

> *I'd like to see Whale Rider. It sounds like an interesting movie.*

The Movies

1 Vocabulary Link

Something old, something new

 A **Pair work.** Pay attention to the words in blue. How are the movies similar? How are they different?

Plot summary: Klara and Alfred work in a gift shop in Budapest, Hungary. They don't like each other. Klara has a pen pal (a man). They don't tell each other their names. Over time, they exchange many letters and fall in love. The funny part: Klara's pen pal is Alfred!

Director: Ernst Lubitsch
Cast: James Stewart, Margaret Sullavan are in the original movie.
Released in 1940

Plot summary: Kathleen owns a small bookstore in New York City. Joe owns a large bookstore nearby. They don't like each other. Joe and Kathleen meet online. They don't tell each other their names. Over time, they fall in love using e-mail.

Director: Nora Ephron
Cast: Tom Hanks and Meg Ryan star in the remake.
Released in 1998

 B Match a word on the left with its definition on the right.

1. __d__ original   a. to be the main actor in a movie
2. _____ remake   b. the story of a movie, book, or play
3. _____ director   c. to make a movie or CD available for people to see or buy
4. _____ cast   d. the first of something, not a copy
5. _____ release   e. all of the actors in a movie or play
6. _____ plot   f. a new version of an old or foreign film
7. _____ star   g. the person in charge of making a movie

 C **Pair work.** Describe a movie you know to a partner. Your partner guesses the title.

Nicole Kidman stars in this movie. It was released in 2004 . . .

Oscar winner

  A Listen to this television interview. Complete the sentences with the correct answer. (CD 2, Track 43)

1. Lauren Swift is an actor / a writer / a director.

2. Lauren won / wants to win an Oscar.

 B Listen again. Lauren is working on a new film now.
Read the sentences and circle *True* or *False*. (CD 2, Track 44)

1. Lauren's new movie is a remake of a 1973 film.	True	False
2. The new film is a romantic comedy.	True	False
3. The original film won an Oscar.	True	False
4. Ewan McGregor and Hugh Grant are going to star in the new film.	True	False
5. The release date for the new movie is next spring.	True	False

ask&
ANSWER
Would you like to see Lauren's new movie?
Why or why not?

World Link

Crouching Tiger, Hidden Dragon (2001) was the first Asian film to be nominated for Best Picture at the Academy Awards. The first South American winner of Best Foreign Film was Argentina's *The Official Story* (1985).

3 Reading

Movie remakes

Do you read movie reviews? If a movie gets a bad review, do you go to see it? Why or why not?

 A Look quickly at the two movie reviews on page 131. Don't read every word. Complete the chart with the information about each movie.

Original movie title	Year	Remake title	Year
	1998	*The Ring*	
Planet of the Apes			

 B Now read the movie reviews more carefully. Then answer the questions that follow.

Reviews of movie remakes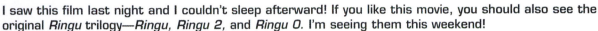

The Ring
Posted by Tia21

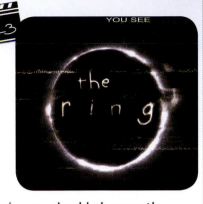

If you want to see a great horror film, rent *The Ring*. Released in 2002, it is a Hollywood remake of the 1998 Japanese horror film, *Ringu*. Like the original, the remake is a very scary movie!

The Ring is the story of a strange videotape. After a person watches it, he or she dies one week later. In the movie, a reporter tries to learn why the tape kills people.

I saw this film last night and I couldn't sleep afterward! If you like this movie, you should also see the original *Ringu* trilogy—*Ringu, Ringu 2,* and *Ringu 0.* I'm seeing them this weekend!

Planet of the Apes
Posted by LukeZ

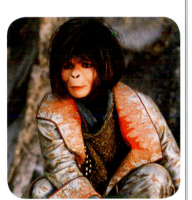

Sometimes, I just don't understand Hollywood. Last night I rented director Tim Burton's remake of *Planet of the Apes.* The 1968 original is a science-fiction classic. The remake has the same name, but it's terrible!

In the original, three men visit a planet controlled by intelligent apes. Humans are like animals. This was an exciting and creative film, and it had an interesting plot.

In the 2001 remake, the special effects are amazing. But the dialog is bad, the plot is confusing, and the film's ending (very important in the original) is silly.

My suggestion: Stay away from Burton's remake and rent the 1968 classic!

 Read the sentences and circle *True* or *False*. If a sentence is false, change it to make it true.

1. *The Ring* is a ~~science-fiction~~ horror film.   True   False

2. *The Ring* is a remake of a Japanese film.   True   False

3. *The Ring* is the story of a strange reporter.   True   False

4. There are three *Ringu* movies.   True   False

5. Luke Z loves the remake of *Planet of the Apes.*   True   False

6. In *Planet of the Apes,* animals visit a planet ruled by apes.   True   False

ask& ANSWER

What is the name of a famous remake you know? Which do you think is better—the original or the remake? Which movies shouldn't be remade? Why?

It is also possible to use *be going to* to talk about future plans:

I'm seeing a movie tonight.
I'm going to see a movie tonight.

A **Pair work.** Read the sentences. Notice how the present continuous is used in each sentence. Then answer the questions with a partner.

a. I'm **seeing** a movie with Ian tonight.
b. After the movie, we're **having** dinner together.
c. Eve is busy. She's **watching** a movie. Can you call later?

1. Which sentence is about something happening now? _____
2. Which sentences are about future plans? _____

B Read the sentences. Underline the present continuous. Then write *N* for something happening now. Write *F* if the sentence talks about a future plan or activity.

1. Let's go! The movie is starting in twenty minutes. __F__
2. I can't see a movie with you tonight. I'm meeting some friends at 8:00. _____
3. Nadia can't go to the movies, either. She's studying for a test in her room. _____
4. Are you meeting Carlos at the café later? _____
5. Why are you calling a cab? I can drive you to the theater now. _____

C **Pair work.** Hal is an actor. Look at his schedule. With a partner, take turns making sentences about his plans. Use the present continuous.

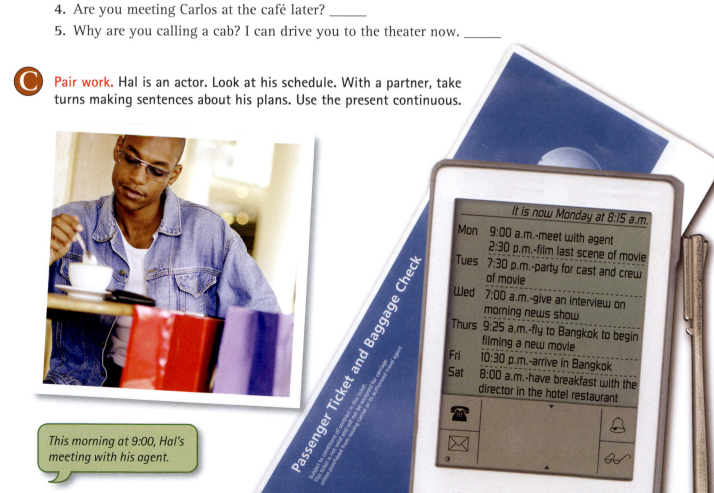

This morning at 9:00, Hal's meeting with his agent.

It is now Monday at 8:15 a.m.
Mon 9:00 a.m.-meet with agent
2:30 p.m.-film last scene of movie
Tues 7:30 p.m.-party for cast and crew of movie
Wed 7:00 a.m.-give an interview on morning news show
Thurs 9:25 a.m.-fly to Bangkok to begin filming a new movie
Fri 10:30 p.m.-arrive in Bangkok
Sat 8:00 a.m.-have breakfast with the director in the hotel restaurant

5 Writing

My favorite movie

 Read the example. Then write about your favorite film of all time on a separate piece of paper

> My favorite movie of all time is Cinema Paradiso. It was released in 1989. It's about a little Italian boy named Salvatore. He loves movies.
>
> In the film, Salvatore remembers his childhood. When he was young, he watched movies at the Cinema Paradiso. He had an old friend named Alfredo. He fell in love with a girl named Elena.
>
> This is a very wonderful and romantic movie!

 Pair work. Exchange papers with a partner. What do you think of your partner's movie choice?

6 Communication

Better the second time?

 Pair work. Work with a partner. Read the directions to do this activity.

1. You and your partner work for a large movie studio. The studio wants to do a movie remake. Together, choose a movie to remake. It can be an old film, a new movie, or a foreign film.

   The movie we are going to remake: _____

   What kind of movie is it? _____

2. How are you going to remake the movie? Complete the chart with your ideas.

Who is going to star in the remake?	
When does the story in the movie take place (in the past, present, future)?	
How is the remake going to be different from the original?	
Are you going to give the remake a new title or use the original title?	

 Group work. Share your ideas with another pair. Listen to their ideas. Do you think your remakes are going to be successful? Why or why not?

 Check out the World Link video. **Practice your English online at http://elt.thomson.com/worldlink**

1 Storyboard

A **Pair work.** Leo and Emma are having lunch in the cafeteria. Look at the pictures and complete the conversations. More than one answer is possible for each blank.

B **Group work.** Practice the conversation with a partner. Then change roles and practice again.

2 See it and say it

 Pair work. Talk about the picture.

- Who are the people in the movie scene?
- What's happening in the scene? How do the people feel?
- What kind of movie is it?
- Who else is on the set of this movie? What are they doing?

In the wedding are the . . .
bride
groom
bridesmaid
best man
minister

 Group work. Get into a group of three or four people.
You are going to perform the movie scene in the picture.

1. Discuss the scene. What's happening? Why do you think it's happening?
2. Choose a person in the scene to role-play.
3. Create a short role play of six to eight sentences. Practice it with your group.

Group work. Role play. Perform your scene for the class.

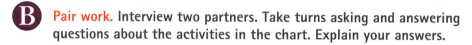

3 Times change

A Look at the activities in the chart below. Add one more idea. Can you do these things now? Could you do them five years ago? Complete the chart with your information. Write *Yes* or *No*.

	Me		Partner 1		Partner 2	
	Now	5 years ago	Now	5 years ago	Now	5 years ago
drive						
speak a second language						
cook simple dishes						
your idea: _____						

B **Pair work.** Interview two partners. Take turns asking and answering questions about the activities in the chart. Explain your answers.

A: Can you drive?
B: Yes, I can. I passed the test last year.
A: Could you drive five years ago?
B: No, I couldn't. I was too young.

C Look at the information in your chart. Which partner are you more similar to? Tell the class.

4 Listening: Survival tips

 A Listen. Tom is talking to a group of students. What are they talking about? Check (✓) the correct answer. (CD 2, Track 45)

☐ how to survive a tornado   ☐ how to survive an earthquake   ☐ how to survive a house fire

 B Listen again. Check (✓) the rules you should follow. (CD 2, Track 46)

1. ☐ Open the windows.
2. ☐ Get under a desk.
3. ☐ Go to the store for food and water.
4. ☐ Don't stand near the walls and windows.
5. ☐ Go outdoors and stand in the street.
6. ☐ Don't use matches.

 C **Pair work.** Have you ever been in an earthquake, a fire, a hurricane, a tornado, or a bad storm? Tell your partner what happened.

> Two years ago, there was a terrible storm in my hometown. My parents and I couldn't leave the house . . .

5 Plans for the day

 A You are going to make an imaginary schedule for tomorrow.
Write five activities from the box on the daily planner.

30 minutes	1 hour	1½ hours	2 hours
go grocery shopping	have your teeth cleaned	clean your apartment	write a paper
get a haircut	work out at the gym	meet a friend for coffee	meet with friends to study

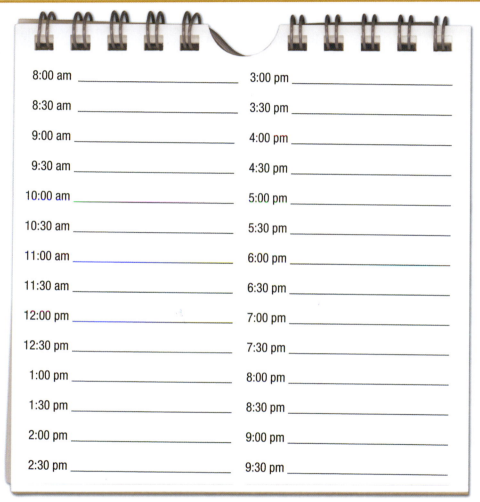

8:00 am _____	3:00 pm _____
8:30 am _____	3:30 pm _____
9:00 am _____	4:00 pm _____
9:30 am _____	4:30 pm _____
10:00 am _____	5:00 pm _____
10:30 am _____	5:30 pm _____
11:00 am _____	6:00 pm _____
11:30 am _____	6:30 pm _____
12:00 pm _____	7:00 pm _____
12:30 pm _____	7:30 pm _____
1:00 pm _____	8:00 pm _____
1:30 pm _____	8:30 pm _____
2:00 pm _____	9:00 pm _____
2:30 pm _____	9:30 pm _____

 B **Pair work.** Think of a fun activity. Then invite your partner.
Agree on a good time and write the activity on your daily planner.

A: What are you doing at 2:00 tomorrow?
B: I'm getting a haircut.
A: How about at 3:00?
B: Nothing. I'm free.
A: Great. Do you want to see a movie?
B: Sure, I'd love to!

C **Pair work.** Think of a different fun activity and invite a new partner to join you.

Language Summaries

Unit 1 *New Friends, New Faces*

Lesson A

Vocabulary Link

age
city
country
e-mail address
first name
interests
languages
last name
occupation

Language Link

Review of the simple present

Speaking

Useful Expressions:
Introducing yourself

My name is Mariana OR
I'm Mariana
    (It's) nice to meet you.
    (It's) nice to meet you, too.

Asking about occupations
What do you do?
    I'm a music student.

Lesson B

Vocabulary Link

age	hairstyle
elderly	curly
in her/his 20s,	long
30s, 40s	short
young	spiky
eye color	straight
blue	height
brown	average height
dark	short
green	tall
hair color	weight
black	average weight
blond	heavyset
gray	slim
light/dark brown	thin
red	

Language Link

Describing people

Unit 2 *Express Yourself!*

Lesson A

Vocabulary Link

angry
bored
embarrassed
happy
nervous
sad
scared

Language Link

Review of the present continuous

Speaking

Useful Expressions:
Asking how someone is

How's it going?
    Great!
    Fine.
    OK/All right.
    So-so.
    Not so good.
    Don't ask!
How're you doing?
    (I'm) fine
    OK.
    So-so.
    I'm stressed.
    I'm tired.
    I'm worried.

Lesson B

Vocabulary Link

bow
call someone
cross one's fingers
kiss
point
shake hands
shrug
wave
wink

Language Link

Object pronouns

Unit 3 *What Do We Need?*

Lesson A

Vocabulary Link

dairy
   cheese
   eggs
   milk
   yogurt
drinks
   juice
   soda
meat and poultry
   beef
   chicken
   ham
produce
   fruit
      apples

bananas
grapes
oranges
vegetables
carrots
corn
lettuce
potatoes
tomatoes
seafood
fish
shrimp

Language Link

Count/Noncount nouns with *some* and *any*

Speaking

Useful Expressions:
Expressing need

Do we need any drinks?
   Yes, we do.
   Yes, we need some.
   No, we don't.
   No, we don't need any.
We need twelve hot dogs.
We need (some) hamburger.

Lesson B

Vocabulary Link

bookstore
department store
drugstore
electronics store
music store
stationery store
toy store

Language Link

some/any, much/many, a lot of

Unit 4 *Around the World*

Lesson A

Vocabulary Link

bank
gym
movie theater
Internet café
laundromat
post office
library
hair salon

Language Link

Prepositions of place

Speaking

Useful Expressions:
Asking for and giving directions

To ask about a specific place:
Excuse me. Where's the Bridge Theater?
   It's on Albany Avenue.
   It's on the corner of Bloor Street
     West and Albany Avenue.

To ask about a place in general:
Is there a movie theater near here?
   Yes, there's one on Albany Avenue.
   No, there isn't.
   Sorry, I don't know.

Lesson B

Vocabulary Link

affordable
cost of living
crime
pollution
population
traffic
transportation
weather

Language Link

How much/How many

Language Summaries

Unit 5 *Vacation!*

Lesson A

Vocabulary Link

clear
cloudy
raining
snowing
sunny
windy

Language Link

Connecting sentences with
but, or, so

Speaking

Useful Expressions:
Giving advice, suggesting

It's chilly in the evening:
    You **should** take a sweater.
    Why don't you take a sweater?
It's snowing:
    You **shouldn't** wear shorts.
    It's not a good idea to drive.

Lesson B

Vocabulary Link

buy a plane ticket
check into your hotel
get a passport
go sightseeing
pack your suitcases
rent a car
show photos to friends
take photos
unpack

Language Link

whose; possessive pronouns;
belong to

Unit 6 *All About You*

Lesson A

Vocabulary Link

baseball
basketball
bowling
chess
rowing
soccer
swimming
tennis
volleyball

Language Link

Verb + noun;
verb + infinitive

Speaking

Useful Expressions:
**Inviting; accepting and declining
invitations**

Do you want to play tennis this afternoon?
    Sure, I'd love to!
    Sorry, I can't. I'm busy.
    Thanks, but . . . (I can't play tennis.)

Lesson B

Vocabulary Link

careful
competitive
creative
hardworking
impulsive
independent
organized
serious

Language Link

How often . . . ?; frequency
expressions

Unit 7 *Change*

Lesson A

Vocabulary Link

get a better job
get a haircut
get in shape
join a club
join a gym
lose weight
make more money
quit smoking

Language Link

Like to vs. *would like to*

Speaking

**Useful Expressions:
Making and responding to requests**

Can I borrow your cell phone? I need to
    call my parents.
Could I borrow . . . ?
Can you lend me . . . ?
Could you lend me . . . ?

Positive responses

Sure. No problem.
Certainly.

Negative responses

I'm sorry, but . . . (+ reason)

Lesson B

Vocabulary Link

become
get married
goal
move
own
successful
take a break

Language Link

The future with *be going to*

Unit 8 *Heroes*

Lesson A

Vocabulary Link

admire
dangerous
evil
hero
intelligent
leader
strong

Language Link

The past tense of *be*

Speaking

**Useful Expressions:
Agreeing and disagreeing**

I think *The Matrix* is a great movie.
    Yeah, I agree.
    Yeah, you're right.
    I think so, too.
    Sorry, but I disagree. In my opinion . . .
    I don't really agree. I think . . .

Lesson B

Vocabulary Link

activist
charities
donate
musician
novelist
peace
talk-show host

Language Link

The simple past: regular verbs

Language Summaries

Unit 9 *The Mind*

Lesson A

Vocabulary Link

believe
forget
memories
memorize
memory
remember
remind

hoc thuoc long

Language Link

The simple past: irregular verbs

Speaking

**Useful Expressions:
Expressing degrees of certainty**

Are the tickets in your desk?
    Yes, they are.
    No, they aren't.

    I think so.
    I don't think so.

    Maybe. I'm not sure.
    I have no idea.

Lesson B

Vocabulary Link

asleep
awake
confusing
daydream
dream
have a nightmare
message
thought
wake up

Language Link

The simple past: question forms

Unit 10 *Your Health*

Lesson A

Vocabulary Link

ankle
arm
chest
ear
eye
finger
foot (feet)
hand
head
leg
mouth
neck
nose
shoulder
stomach
toe
tooth (teeth)

Language Link

The imperative

Speaking

**Useful Expressions:
Talking about health problems**

What's wrong?
What's the matter?
    I don't feel well.
    I'm sick.
    I have a(n) . . .
    My . . . hurts

Lesson B

Vocabulary Link

calm
down
energetic
energy
exhausted
reduce
stressed

Language Link

When-clauses

Unit 11 *That's Amazing*

Lesson A

Vocabulary Link

champion
compete
inventor
magician
talent
talented
trick
wiz

Language Link

Talking about skills and talents with *can* and *could*

Speaking

Useful Expressions:
Offering compliments

This/Your . . . is very interesting/beautiful/
  smart.
That's a nice/cool . . .
I like this/your . . . a lot.
You can . . . really well.

Accepting compliments

Thank you.
Thanks.
That's nice of you to say.

Lesson B

Vocabulary Link

achievements
amazing
confident
give up
journey
survive

Language Link

Connecting ideas with *because*

Unit 12 *The Movies*

Lesson A

Vocabulary Link

action/adventure
animation
comedy
drama
horror
musical
romance
science fiction (sci-fi)

Language Link

-ing/-ed adjectives

Speaking

Useful Expressions:
Telephoning

Hello? Is Michael there?
  Who's calling?
This is Silvio.
  OK. Hang on a minute.
  Sorry. Michael isn't here. Can I take a
    message?

Lesson B

Vocabulary link

cast
director
original
plot
release
remake
star

Language Link

The present continuous as future

Grammar Notes

Unit 1 *New Friends, New Faces*

Lesson A

Language Link: Review of the simple present

Yes/No questions with *be*	Positive responses	Negative responses
Am I in this class?	Yes, you are (in this class).	No, you're not (in this class). No, you aren't (in this class).
Are you a student?	Yes, I am (a student).	No, I'm not (a student).
Are they students?	Yes, they are (students).	No, they're not (students). No, they aren't (students).
Is he a student?	Yes, he is (a student).	No, he's not (a student). No, he isn't (a student).

Yes/No questions with other verbs	Positive responses	Negative responses
Do you speak English?	Yes. I speak English. Yes, I do.	No, I don't (speak English).
Does he speak Italian?	Yes, he speaks Italian. Yes, he does.	No, he doesn't (speak Italian).

Wh-questions				
Wh-word	*Do/Does*	Subject	Verb	
Where	do	you	live?	(I live) in London, England.
	does	she		(She lives) in São Paulo, Brazil.
What	do	you	do on the weekend?	I go out with my friends.
	does	she		She spends time with her family.

Lesson B

Language Link: Describing people

What does he look like?	
Be + adjective	*Have* + (adjective) noun
Peter is tall. He's 182 cm. He is average weight. He's clean-shaven. He's in his twenties. He's young.	Carlos has brown eyes. He has black, curly hair. He has a beard and a mustache.

Unit 2 *Express Yourself!*

Lesson A

Language Link: Review of the present continuous

	Subject	*Be*	Verb-*ing*
Positive	I	am	smiling.
	You	are	
	He/She	is	
	We	are	
	They	are	

	Subject	*Be*	*Not*	Verb-*ing*
Negative	I	am	not	listening.
	You	are		
	He/She	is		
	We	are		
	They	are		

Yes/No questions

Be	Subject	Verb-*ing*	Positive response	Negative response
Are	you they	listening?	Yes, I am (listening). Yes, they are (listening).	No, I'm not (listening). No, they aren't (listening).
Is	he/she		Yes, he/she is (listening).	No, he/she isn't (listening).

Wh-questions

Wh-word	*Be*	Subject	Verb-*ing*		
What	are	you	doing?	I'm reading.	
	is	he/she		He/She's talking on the phone.	

Lesson B

Language Link: Object pronouns

Subject pronouns	Verb	Object	
I/You/We/They	know like	Mary.	• In English, many sentences have a subject, a verb, and an object. • A direct object answers the question *Who* or *What*?
He/She/It	knows likes	Korean food.	

Subject	Verb	Object pronouns	
Carlos	knows	me/you/him/her/ it/us/them.	• In a sentence, the object can be a pronoun: Carlos knows **Mary**. Maya likes **my parents**. He knows **her**. She likes **them**.

Unit 3 *What Do We Need?*

Lesson A

Language Link: Count/Noncount nouns with *some* and *any*

Count nouns		Noncount nouns
singular	plural	
a chicken (the whole chicken) an orange	two chickens two oranges	beef milk water

- In English, there are **count nouns** and **noncount nouns**.
- Noncount nouns don't use *a*, *an*, or a number in front of the noun.
- Noncount nouns are always singular.

Count/Noncount nouns with *some* and *any*

	Question	Positive answer	Negative answer
Noncount nouns	Do we have **any** lettuce?	Yes, we have **some** (lettuce).	No, we don't have **any** (lettuce).
Plural count nouns	Do we have **any** potatoes?	Yes, we have some (potatoes). Yes, we have three (potatoes).	No, we don't have **any** (potatoes).

- Use *any* in questions with noncount nouns and plural count nouns.
- Use *any* in negative statements with noncount nouns and plural count nouns.
- Use *some* in statements with noncount nouns and plural count nouns.

Measure words

Measure words	Noncount nouns	
a cup of	coffee/tea	With many noncount nouns, we use measure words. These measure words make an item countable.
a bottle of	water	
a glass of	milk/water/juice/water	Mary drinks *coffee* every day.
a loaf of	bread	Mary drinks *two cups of coffee* every day.
a piece of	chicken/beef/ham	
a head of	lettuce	Please buy *some bread*.
a bar of	soap	Please buy *two loaves of bread*.
a tube of	toothpaste	

Lesson B

Language Link:

Quantifiers—*some/ any, much/many, a lot of*

	Noncount nouns			Count nouns		
Positive	There's	**a lot of** some	clothing. jewelry.	There are	**a lot of** some	shoes. hats.
Negative	There isn't	**much** any	furniture. software.	There aren't	**many** any	books. toys.

Unit 4 *Around the World*

Lesson A

Language Link: Prepositions of place

> ### Prepositions of place
>
> There is a drugstore **on the corner.**
> Let's meet this evening at the Moonlight Café **on** Seventh Avenue.
> The café is **next to** the drugstore.
> There's a bus stop **in front of** a Mexican restaurant on Seventh.
> It's **in the middle of** the block, **between** a gas station and a gym.

Lesson B

Language Link: *How much/How many*

How much/How many with count nouns	
How many restaurants are there in your neighborhood?	There are **a lot/some/two.** There **aren't many.** There's one or two. There **aren't any.**/There are **none.**
With noncount nouns	
How much traffic is there in your city?	There's **a lot/some.** There's **a little.**/There **isn't much.** There **isn't any.**/There's **none.**

Unit 5 *Vacation!*

Lesson A

Language Link: Connecting sentences with *but, or, so*

Connecting sentences, words, and phrases with *but, or, so*	
It's cold in Boston, **but** it's warm in Miami. It's cold **but** sunny in Vancouver today. It's a nice day **but** a little hot.	*But* shows an opposite idea or contrast. *But* joins words, phrases, and sentences.
We can go to the beach, **or** we can visit the zoo. Is it warm **or** chilly today? I'm in a hurry! I can't stop to talk **or** to take a break.	*Or* gives a choice. *Or* joins words, phrases, and sentences.
It's raining, **so** we're not having a picnic in the park.	*So* gives a result. *So* joins sentences.

Lesson B

Language Link: *Whose*; possessive pronouns; *belong to*

	Possessive adjectives	Possessive pronouns	*belongs to*
Whose passport is this?	It's **my** passport. **your** **her** **his** **our** **their**	It's **mine**. **yours**. **hers**. **his**. **ours**. **theirs**	It belongs to **me**. **you**. **her**. **him**. **us**. **them**.

- *Whose* and *who's* have the same pronunciation, but different meanings.
- *Whose* asks about the owner of something, for example:
  Whose house is this?
- *Who's* is a contraction of *Who* and *is*: Who's studying English?

Unit 6 *All About You*

Lesson A

Language Link: Verb + noun; verb + infinitive

Verb + noun	
I love **baseball**. It's my favorite sport. I want **a new car**. I don't like **spicy food**. Do you like **country music**?	A **noun** or **noun phrase** can follow many verbs.
Verb + infinitive	
I love **to play** tennis. I want **to buy** a new car. She doesn't like **to eat** spicy food. Do you plan **to visit** Australia?	The **infinitive** is *to* + the base form of a verb. The **infinitive** can follow certain verbs. Some of these are *like, love, hate, want, plan*, and *expect*.

Lesson B

Language Link: *How often . . . ?*; frequency expressions

How often do you check your e-mail?	(I check my e-mail) **every day/Monday/week/month**. **all the time**. (very often) **once a week**. **twice a month**. **three times a year**. **once in a while**. (not very often) I **never** check my e-mail. I don't have a computer!

- *How often* asks about the frequency of an event.
- Don't use *How often* with the present continuous.
- Expressions of frequency (*every day, once in a while*) usually come at the end of a sentence. Sometimes they come at the beginning.

Unit 7 Change

Lesson A

Language Link: *Like to* vs. *would like to*

- The following sentence means *I enjoy visiting Australia*. It states a fact about the present:
  I **like to** visit Australia. My favorite place is Bondi Beach.

- The following sentence means *I want to visit Australia next summer*:
  I**'d like to** visit Australia next summer.

- Use *I'd like to . . .* to state a future hope or desire.

- The following sentence means *Do you want to visit Australia?*
  Would you like to visit Australia?

- You can use *Would you like to* + verb to ask about a future hope or desire.

Note these contracted forms:

I'd	–	I would	**he'd**	–	he would	**we'd**	–	we would
you'd	–	you would	**she'd**	–	she would	**they'd**	–	they would

Lesson B

Language Link: The future with *be going to*.

Subject + *be*		*Going to*	Verb		Future time expressions
I'm You're He's/She's We're They're	not	going to	visit	Mexico	tomorrow. this summer. next month/year/summer. in two years. after graduation.

- Use *be going to* to talk about future plans:
  I'm going to visit Mexico next month.
- Use *be going to* to make predictions:
  Don't worry. You're going to do great on the test!
- *Going to* is often said as "gonna." Don't use "gonna" in writing.

Yes/No questions	Are you going to visit Mexico this summer? Yes, I am. Yes, maybe. No, I'm not.
Wh-questions	What are you going to do this summer? I'm going to visit Mexico.

Unit 8 *Heroes*

Lesson A

Language Link: The past tense of *be*

Subject	*Be*		
I He/She	was **wasn't**	famous in Toronto	last year/summer. in 1984. twenty years ago.
You We They	were **weren't**		

Yes/No **questions**	Were you born in Mexico?
	    Yes, I was.
	    No, I wasn't. I was born in Chile.

Wh-questions

Where was Marie Curie born?	(She was born) In Warsaw.
What was her occupation?	(She was a) Scientist.
Who was she married to?	(She was married to) Pierre Curie.
When were they married?	(They were married) In 1895.
Why was she famous?	She was the first person to win a Nobel Prize twice.

Lesson B

Language Link: The simple past—regular verbs

The simple past tense: regular verbs			
I You He/She We They	visited **didn't visit**	Mexico last month.	In the past tense, the verb form is the same for all persons To form the negative, use *did not* or *didn't* + the base form of the verb.

The simple past tense of regular verbs: spelling rules	
mov**e** -> mov**ed**	If the verb ends in *e* add *d*.
visi**t** -> visi**ted**	If the verb ends with a consonant, add *ed*.
s**top** -> sto**pped**	With one-syllable verbs that end with a consonant-vowel-consonant, double the last letter and add *ed*.
stud**y** -> stud**ied**	If the word ends in consonant + *y*, change the *y* to *i* and add *ed*.
pl**ay** -> pl**ayed**	If the word ends with vowel + *y*, add *ed*.

Unit 9 *The Mind*

Lesson A

Language Link: The simple past—irregular verbs

<table>
<tr><td colspan="2" align="center">The simple past: irregular verbs</td></tr>
<tr>
<td>
I
You
He/She   **forgot** the tickets at home.
We   **didn't forget** the tickets at home.
They
</td>
<td>
Do not add *ed* to irregular past tense verbs in positive statements. See the list of irregular verbs below.

To form the negative, use *did not* or *didn't* + the base form of the verb.
</td>
</tr>
</table>

Base form	Past tense	Base form	Past tense
begin	began	go	went
bring	brought	have	had
buy	bought	know	knew
come	came	make	made
do	did	run	ran
drink	drank	say	said
eat	ate	shake	shook
fall	fell	speak	spoke
feel	felt	take	took
forget	forgot	teach	taught
get	got	think	thought
give	gave	win	won

Lesson B

Language Link: The simple past—question forms

	Yes/No questions	Answers
Regular verbs	**Did you study** for the test?	Yes, I **did.** Yes, I **studied** for the test. No, I **didn't.** No, I **didn't study** for the test.
Irregular verbs	**Did you forget** the tickets?	Yes, I **did.** Yes, I **forgot** the tickets. No, I **didn't.** No, I **didn't forget** the tickets.

	Wh-questions	Answers
Regular verbs	**When did** you **study**?	(I studied) last night.
Irregular verbs	**Where did** you **forget** the tickets?	(I forgot them) at home.

Unit 10 *Your Health*

Lesson A

Language Link: The imperative

In an imperative statement, the subject is always *you*, but we don't write or say it:

Relax for an hour. You're tired.
Don't work so hard.

The imperative uses the base form of the verb. In the negative, use *don't* + the base form of the verb.

Use the imperative to give advice:

Relax for an hour. You're tired.

Use the imperative to give instructions:

Take this medicine twice a day.
Don't drive when you take this medicine.

Use the imperative to give directions:

Go two blocks and **turn** left.

Use the imperative to give commands and orders:

Be quiet!

Use the imperative to make requests:

Close the window, please.
Don't smoke in here, please.

Lesson B

Language Link: *When*-clauses

When-clause	Result clause
When(ever) I drink a lot of coffee,	I can't sleep.
When(ever) I see sad movies,	I cry.

- These sentences talk about things that are usually true: *When X happens, Y is the result.*
- In the *when*-clause, you can also use the word *whenever*.
- The present tense is used in the *when*-clause and in the result clause.

Result clause	*When*-clause
I can't sleep	when(ever) I drink a lot of coffee.

- The result can come first in a sentence. In this case, there is no comma between the result and the *when*-clause.

Unit 11 *That's Amazing*

Lesson A

Language Link: Talking about skills and talents with *can* and *could*

Talking about skills and talents with *can* and *could*		
Can you speak Spanish?	Yes, I **can**. No, I **can't**.	• Use *can* to talk about skills, abilities, and talents in the present.
Who can speak French?	Naoki **can**. My parents **can't**.	
Could you speak Spanish as a child?	Yes, I **could**. No, I **couldn't**.	• *Could* is the past tense of *can*.
Who could read at age 2?	Monika **could**. Jackie **couldn't**.	• *Can* and *could* use the same form in all persons.

Lesson B

Language Link: Connecting ideas with *because*

Main clause   **Reason clause**

I'm hungry   **because I didn't eat breakfast.**
- *Because* joins two sentences together. It comes at the beginning of the reason clause.
- *Because* answers the question *why*; it gives a reason.
- To answer questions in conversation, people often give the reason only. Please note that this style is not correct for formal, written English:
  A: Why are you hungry? **B: Because** I didn't eat breakfast.

Reason clause   **Main clause**

Because I didn't eat breakfast,   I'm hungry.
- The reason can also come first in a sentence. In this case, put a comma between the reason and the main clause.

Unit 12 *The Movies*

Lesson A

Language Link: *-ing/-ed* adjectives

- Adjectives ending in *-ed* and *-ing* describe people, things, or situations:

  I'm **interested** in Ridley Scott's movies.
  Ridley Scott's movies are **interesting**.
  Ridley Scott is (an) **interesting** (director).

- Adjectives ending in *-ed* usually describe a person's emotions: how he or she feels. Adjectives ending in *-ing* describe people or things that cause a feeling:

  I'm **bored** because this movie is **boring**.
  I was **confused** because the story was **confusing**.

Lesson B

Language Link: The present continuous as future

- The present continuous (subject + *be* + verb + *-ing*) can be used to talk about actions happening now or these days and also to talk about future plans:

    Eve **is sleeping** now. Can you call later?   I'm **seeing** a movie with Ian at 7:30.
    Mick **is studying** at UCLA this summer.   After the movie, we**'re having** dinner together.

- It is possible to use the present continuous or *be going to* to talk about future plans:

    I'm **having** dinner with Ian tonight.   I'm **going to have** dinner with Ian tonight.

- We do not usually use the present progressive with *stative* verbs, for example: *be, love, hate, (dis)like, want, need, know, think, have.*

Answers

Page 11, 6. Communication, Activity A

Answers: 1. f, **2.** e, **3.** d, **4.** c, **5.** b, **6.** a

Page 65, 6. Communication, Activity B

Personality Type 1	Personality Type 2	Personality Type 3	Personality Type 4
You care about other people. You want to help them. But sometimes, you're too picky! Remember, people aren't perfect.	You're hardworking and want to be successful. But remember—it's important to smile. Don't be so serious all the time!	You love to learn and try new things. You're also very smart. But sometimes, you're too competitive. Let others win once in a while!	You're interesting, and you love adventure. But be careful! Sometimes you're very impulsive! Remember to think about your future, too!

Page 84, 6. Communication, Activity B

Answer: Cleopatra VII, the last pharaoh of Egypt